The WELL DRESSED *Bear*

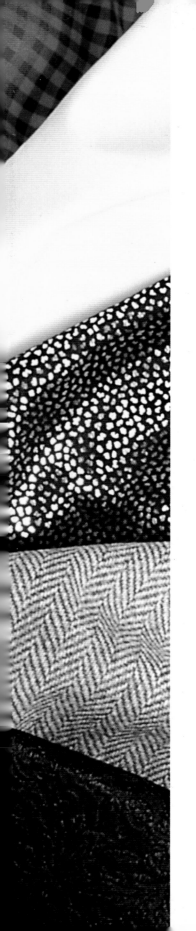
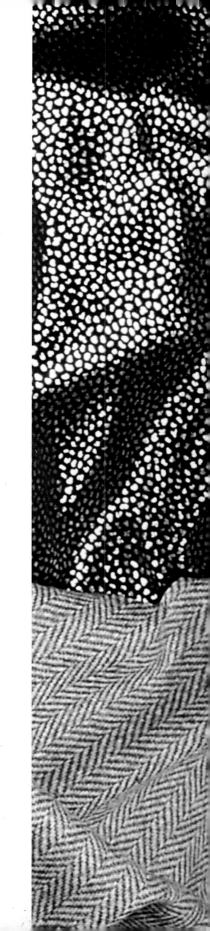

The
WELL DRESSED
Bear

Geraldine Thistlethwaite

WEIDENFELD
& NICOLSON

LONDON

Contents

Introduction

Why do some bears wear clothes and others don't? As in most things, this is purely a matter of choice for you or for your bear. If you favour the first option, and want to ensure that your bear is properly dressed whatever the occasion, this book will provide you with a complete wardrobe of outfits and many happy hours spent making and using them. The bears featured in this book have been especially made by Pam Howells, one of the most respected bear-makers today. The gentleman is 51cm (20in) tall and the lady is 40.5cm (16in) tall. The diagrams below give additional measurements, and there is advice about fit on page 83.

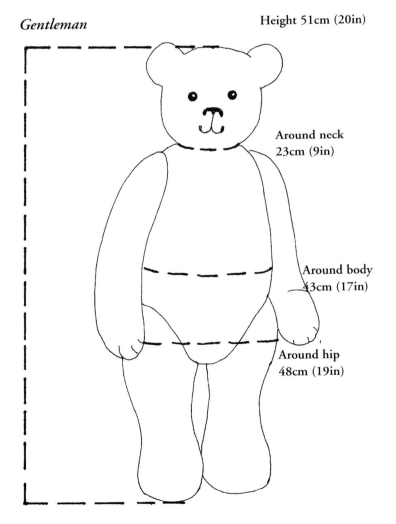

Gentleman

Height 51cm (20in)

Around neck
23cm (9in)

Around body
43cm (17in)

Around hip
48cm (19in)

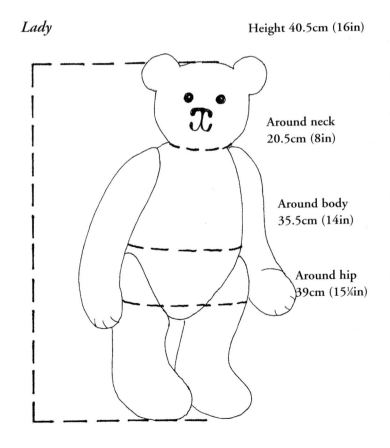

Lady

Height 40.5cm (16in)

Around neck
20.5cm (8in)

Around body
35.5cm (14in)

Around hip
39cm (15¼in)

Equipment

Very little equipment is necessary for the projects in this book. You need two pairs of scissors – a pair of standard 20cm (8in) general-purpose scissors for cutting out fabric, and a pair of sharp pointed scissors for snipping into corners and buttonholes. Make sure that you reserve both pairs for sewing only. It is incredibly difficult to cut fabrics and threads once the blades have been blunted by paper or cardboard.

In addition, you will need some fine dressmakers' pins, tacking thread (cotton thread that isn't shiny), general-purpose needles and a tape measure. Also useful are a pincushion and a seam ripper, or 'quick unpick'. An iron is vital, along with a pressing cloth for any damp pressing required, depending on your choice of fabric. To make the pattern pieces, you will need good-quality tracing paper.

Don't worry if you have no sewing machine. All the garments can be made totally by hand, using backstitch instead of machine stitch.

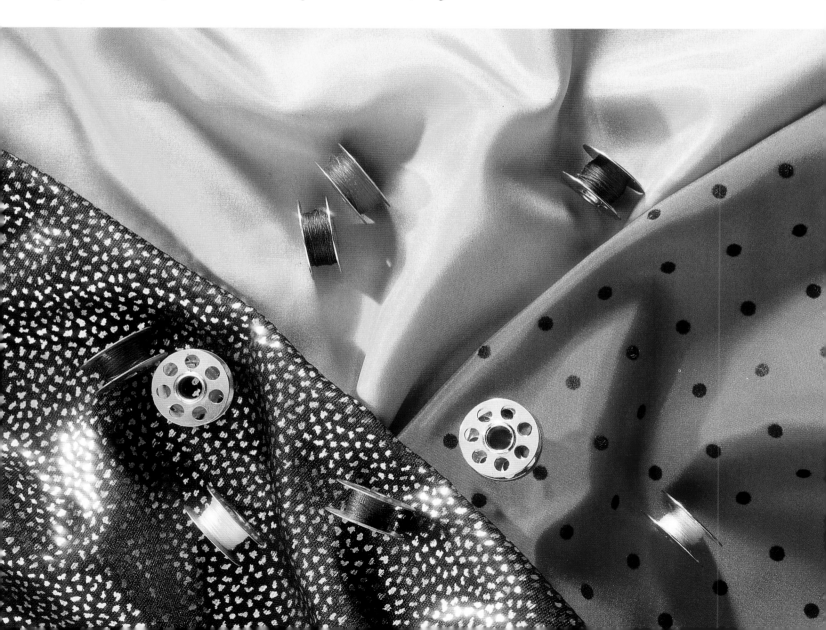

Choosing Fabrics

The next thing to consider when thinking about a particular garment is the fabric to be used, and visiting a good fabric store can fill one with delight at all the possibilities, as well as confusion as to where to begin. However, there are certain considerations to be borne in mind which will help you to make a suitable final choice.

You will be looking not only for a colour that flatters, but also for a printed or woven pattern suitable in scale for the size of the garment. A large-scale check may only show a fraction of its colour range and repeat on

the finished garment. Choose instead a small-scale check.

A thick tweed can cause dreadful problems with bulk, and you can end up with hems like motor tyres and collars that are impossible to roll. Choose a tweed whose thickness is appropriate to the scale of the garment. Another pointer is that very loosely woven fabrics are, generally speaking, unsuitable for bears' garments that have a fair amount of tailoring.

Finally, always keep in mind that fabrics which might on a human scale seem

unpromising become wonderful prospects when considered from a bear's outlook.

Always try to buy the best fabrics you can afford, as they generally handle better than very cheap fabrics. If you are a complete beginner, it might be better to avoid fine silks, chiffons, crêpes and velvets at first, as these are not always the easiest to handle – they fray, slip, slide and walk! As you gain experience, or if you are already an experienced dressmaker, they should not pose a problem.

Make a note, too, of the manufacturer's fabric care and cleaning recommendations. When buying fusible interfacing, ensure that the cleaning requirements (washing, dry cleaning, etc) match those of the fabric.

On the subject of old and antique fabrics, I prefer to use new every time. An antique look is easily achieved by the judicious choice of style and fabric. However, there are times when it may be more appropriate to use an older fabric, but do make sure that it is clean and sound.

Techniques

MAKING THE PATTERN PIECES

1 Use the templates at the back of the book to make the patterns. Carefully trace the shapes and markings onto tracing paper, then have the tracing enlarged on a photocopier. Unless otherwise indicated, each dimension should be doubled. (If you do not have access to a photocopier, draw a grid on your tracing, draw another grid to the required enlargement on a piece of paper and then transfer the pattern to the paper, square by square.)

2 Cut out the pattern pieces, cutting *on* the lines rather than around them; even quite small variations can cause the garments to fit badly. Once you have cut out all the pieces make sure you keep them together in a place where you are sure they can't get damaged or lost. Pay particular attention to the smaller pieces as tehy have a habit of being mislaid or getting confused with pieces from other patterns.

PREPARING THE FABRIC

3 Before cutting out the fabric itself, you will need to straighten the cut ends and make sure that it hangs true. If the fabric has become distorted during manufacture, even small garments like bears' clothes will hang badly unless you straighten it. At one end of the fabric length, make a snip across the selvedge. (The selvedges are the finished edges running lengthwise along each side.) Tease a single crosswise thread free and gently pull it to create puckering along the cut edge. Cut the fabric along the puckered thread line. Repeat at the other end.

4 Fold the fabric in half along the straight of grain (parallel to the lengthwise threads

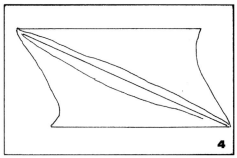

and selvedges). The cut ends should be even at both ends, the selvedges should line up and the fabric should lie flat without puckering. If this is not the case, you must even up the weave by pulling diagonally opposite corners of the fabric in opposite directions. If this doesn't square up the fabric, take the other two corners and pull again. Persevere with this until you are satisfied that the fabric is as even as you can make it.

CUTTING OUT

5 All the pattern pieces are cut on double-thickness fabric unless otherwise directed. Fold the fabric along the straight of grain. The correct seam allowances have been included in each pattern piece, so the lines shown are the cutting lines. You will therefore be able to place the pattern pieces very closely together on the fabric.

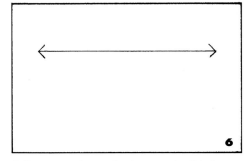

6 Be sure to lay each piece on the fabric

with the pattern's straight-of-grain line exactly on the straight of grain of the fabric. You can check this by measuring from the line on the pattern to the selvedge.

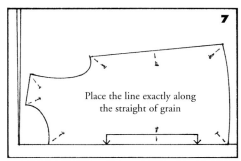

Place the line exactly along the straight of grain

7 If a pattern has a foldline marked along one edge, the pattern is for only half of the piece. Place the foldline along the fold of the fabric so that when the pattern piece is cut out the two layers will unfold to become one fabric piece.

8 Pin first along the straight of grain line, or along the foldline if any, then just inside the cutting lines, pinning through both layers of fabric. Avoid using too many pins, which would distort the pattern and fabric.

9 When cutting out, place your free hand gently on the pinned area to ensure that the fabric beneath the pattern does not slide away from the scissors blades, or distort. Do not lift the fabric while cutting.

TRANSFERRING THE PATTERN MARKINGS

10 Leave the pattern pieces pinned to the cut fabric. Transfer all the pattern markings except for the straight of grain markings (which are used only for positioning – see step 6) using tailor tacks and running tailor tacks (see steps 11 and 12).

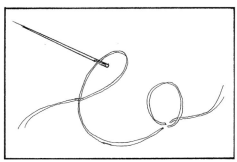

11 To make tailor tacks, thread your hand-sewing needle with a long double strand of thread. Insert the needle into the fabric from the side facing you, and take a small return stitch to that same side, leaving a short length of thread hanging free at the entry point. Make a second stitch exactly as the first, and in the same position, but leave a loop of thread between the entry and exit point. Snip your threaded end free, leaving a tail, and snip the centre of the loop. When you eventually separate the layers, snip the threads between the layers, so that both fabric pieces are marked with a small tuft of thread.

12 Running tailor tacks, which are used to mark hemlines, are simpler. Again, thread the needle with a long double strand, and then make 1.25cm (½in) running stitches, leaving all the stitches on the side facing you as loops. Cut the loops, and then proceed as for step 11.

13 While it is easier to do all the tailor tacking required for a garment at once, it is better to remove each pattern piece from the fabric only when that piece is ready to be sewn. This helps keep the fabric clean and the pieces recognizable and safe.

14 When you do remove the pattern pieces, if there is no discernible difference between the right and wrong sides of the fabric, put a pin in the right side of each piece as the pattern is removed.

15 Don't be tempted to take short cuts by using methods other than those given for a specific garment, or by omitting the tacking. Tacking ensures that the fabric pieces will hold steady at the required area, so that the machine pressure, or hand pressure when sewing the seam, will not cause the fabric to stretch unevenly or slip away. Using a different construction method from the given method can actually make further construction of that garment difficult. Short cuts usually prove a longer way round and may spoil the garment.

16 Stitch each seam with a machine stitch or a hand backstitch. The seam allowances are 6mm (¼in) unless otherwise stated. Take care to secure each end of the stitching by either tying the two ends by hand or backstitching the ends into the stitching.

17 For the majority of seams in this book, the instructions say to stitch again just inside the first stitching to strengthen the seam. The seam allowances are then trimmed, and zigzagged together, but the instructions will specify this. On fabric that is very loosely woven or frays easily, take care not to trim off too much fabric from seams with only a single row of stitching. The stitches must be able to bind the layers together, and over-zealous trimming on these fabrics may cause your seams to deconstruct! Using a smaller stitch at stress areas, such as collar points, is a good precaution when using these fabrics.

18 Don't forget that when you turn a garment piece right side out, the enclosed raw edges will cause a certain amount of ridging and bulk. Eliminate some of this by trimming excess fabric from the allowances and then trimming the less important seam allowance (such as a facing) so it is slightly narrower than the other. This is called layering.

19 Having trimmed the curves, notch or clip the allowances so that the curves lie flat and smooth. An outward curve is clipped, while an inward curve, such as a neckline, is notched. A notch is a small V-shaped cut in the seam allowance, which will prevent a fabric from bunching.

20 Similarly, when turning a corner or sewing a collar tip, the seam allowance is trimmed as close to the stitching as possible, to prevent the corner from puckering making it neat and even. Instructions for reinforcing corners before trimming and turning are given where relevant.

21 Everyone makes mistakes, particularly when tired or in a hurry. Try to avoid unpicking a mistake at night – wait until the morning. You may find that you have not made a mistake after all.

22 Pressing is recommended throughout. It may seem boring, time-consuming and unnecessary, but careful pressing at every stage is an integral part of the process. It promotes accurate handling and fit and gives a professional finish. If you proceed steadily and carefully with each stage of the garment, tasks like pressing, which may initially seem irksome, will become part of the pleasure of the making.

Gentleman's
DRESSING GOWN AND SLIPPERS

The dressing gown is made from polyester/wool worsted. Trimmed at the cuffs, pockets, collar and both sides of the front with contrasting piping, it is tied at the waist with a cord. The lined slippers are velvet, and have contrasting soles and gentlemanly trims to the tops. To reduce bulk and preserve the softness of the garment, the piping is sewn onto the dressing gown by hand instead of being encased in the seam, and interfacing is omitted from the collar, cuffs, pockets and facings.

FABRIC REQUIREMENTS

FABRIC WIDTH	90cm (36in)	115cm (45in)	136cm (54in)	150cm (60in)
DRESSING GOWN	70cm (¾yd)	70cm (¾yd)	70cm (¾yd)	70cm (¾yd)
SLIPPERS VELVET	30cm (¼yd)	30cm (¼yd)	30cm (¼yd)	30cm (¼yd)
SLIPPERS LINING	30cm (¼yd)	30cm (¼yd)	30cm (¼yd)	30cm (¼yd)

TO FINISH

DRESSING GOWN	3mm (⅛in) wide piping cord: 3.2m (3½yd) • Matching sewing thread
SLIPPERS	20.5cm (8in) square of contrasting poplin • Scrap of dressing gown fabric • Matching sewing thread • 2 buttons

See page 88–90 for pattern templates

PREPARATION

Pin the pattern pieces onto the prepared fabric as directed on the pattern. Cut the pieces out. Transfer all markings from the pattern pieces to the fabric using tailor tacks and long running tailor tacks.

The dressing gown

POCKET

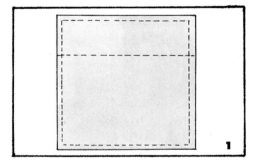

1 Stitch 6mm (¼in) from the edges of each pocket piece. Zigzag all the raw edges. Press.

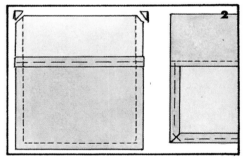

2 At the top edge of each pocket, turn under 6mm (¼in); press and tack. Fold the flap to the right side along the marked foldline. Pin, tack and stitch a 6mm (¼in) seam along both side edges, from the top to the turned-under edge. Trim off the corners. Turn the flap back to the wrong side, and press. Turn under 6mm (¼in) on the remaining raw edges; tack, mitring the corners. Press. On the wrong side, machine stitch the hem flap to the pocket, close to the tacked edge. Remove the tacking and press the pocket.

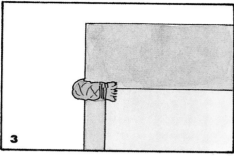

3 Hand sew piping across the pocket fronts, using the machine stitching across the pocket top as a guide. Curve the ends around to the wrong side, secure firmly and cut. Pin and tack the pockets to the two front pieces, matching the pocket corners to the tailor tacks. Hand sew in place. Remove the tacking and the tailor tacks. Press.

JOINING THE FRONT AND BACK

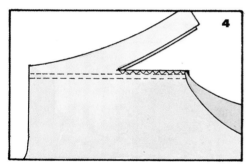

4 With right sides together, join the front and back sections together at both shoulder seams, taking 6mm (¼in) seams. Stitch again just inside the first line of stitching. Press to sink the stitches into the fabric. Trim the seams close to the stitching and zigzag the raw edges together. Press the seams towards the back.

FACINGS AND COLLAR

5 With right sides together, join the facing/collar sections at the centre back. Press the seam open.

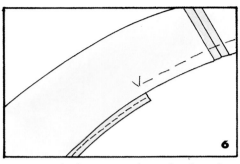

6 Zigzag the long, curved, inside edge of the facing. Turn under 6mm (¼in) on this edge, tack and stitch. Remove the tacking and press.

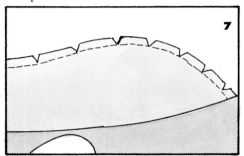

7 Zigzag any curved edges of the undercollar that are likely to fray during handling. With right sides together, pin and tack the neck edge of the undercollar to the neck edge of the garment, matching centre backs, shoulders and tailor tacks; stitch. With the tip of the iron, carefully press the seam open flat, clipping into the seam allowance on the curves.

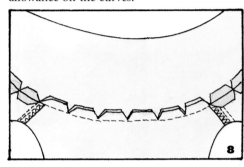

8 Between the shoulder seams, press the seam back up towards the neck edge, leaving the seam open on either side.

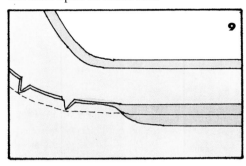

9 With right sides together, pin, tack and stitch the facing/collar section to the undercollar and garment fronts, matching the markings. Remove the tacking. Press, clipping the curves. Press the facing seam back to the garment. Turn the facings to the wrong side and press. Pin them to the garment as far as the shoulder seams.

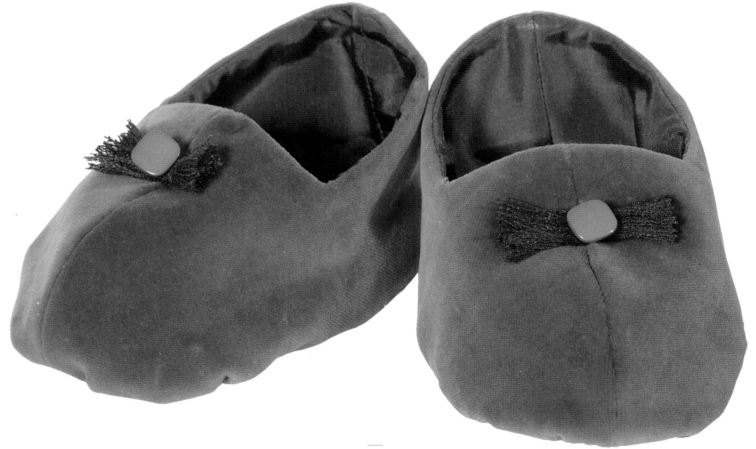

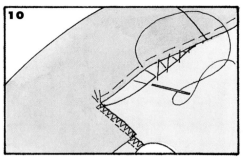

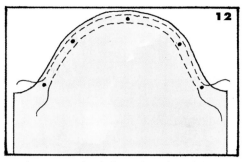

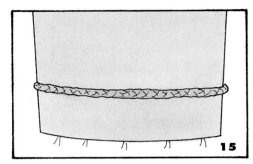

10 Clip the neck edge of the overcollar at the tailor tacks. Turn under along the marked line and tack. Slipstitch the tacked edge to the neckline seam. Press. Lay the remaining raw edge over the shoulder seamline. Catch into place and finish the raw edges by hand. Press.

CUFFS

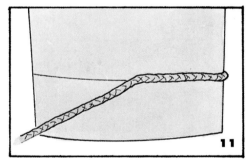

11 With right sides together, pin, tack and stitch one long unmarked cuff section to the bottom edge of each sleeve. Remove the tacking. Press the seam open and then up towards the sleeve top. Zigzag stitch the bottom edge of the cuff. Turn the sleeve over to the right side, lay piping along the seamline and hand sew into place.

SLEEVES

12 Make two lines of running stitches within the seam allowance between the tailor tacks on the sleeve head. With right sides together, pin and tack the sleeve head into the armhole section of the garment, matching the tailor tacks and easing the fabric between the marks so it will fit smoothly. Stitch the whole armhole seam,

stitching 1cm (⅜in) from the edge of the armhole. Remove all the tacking. Stitch again just inside the first line of stitching. Trim the excess fabric away, close to the stitching, and zigzag the stitched edge. Press the stitching using the tip of an iron.

13 With right sides together, pin, tack and stitch the sleeve and body side seams together, making sure the armhole seamline faces down towards the sleeve edge. Stitch again just inside the first line of stitching. Press. Trim away excess fabric close to the stitching. Zigzag the raw edges together. Press the seam flat, then press the entire seam towards the back of the garment.

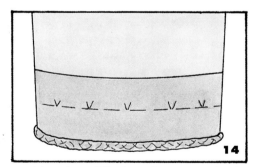

14 Turn the cuff back to the wrong side of the sleeve so that the piping runs along the bottom edge of the sleeve. Tack the two layers together along the foldline.

15 Turn the sleeve to the right side again. Overlap the cuff back onto the sleeve, so that the foldline is at the bottom edge of the sleeve. Tack through all thicknesses around the edge.

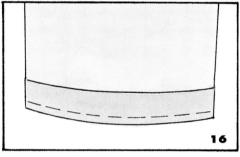

16 Turn the sleeve back to the wrong side and herringbone stitch the raw edge to the sleeve, taking care not to catch in the outer cuff. Finally, on the right side, catch the cuff to the sleeve at the sleeve seam, just below the piping. Remove all the tacking; press. Repeat for the other sleeve.

HEM AND FINISHING

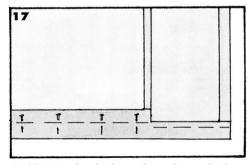

17 Turn under the hem along the marked hemline on the garment lower edge. Pin and tack. Cut 6mm (¼in) from the facing area, in order to reduce bulk; overcast the new raw edge. Herringbone stitch the hem to the garment. Press.

18 Starting at the bottom right front, insert the end of the piping cord between the front edge and the facing. Secure it firmly and then hand stitch the cord in place, continuing up the front edge, around the collar and back down the other front edge. Secure this end too between the garment and the facing. Slipstitch the facings back onto the hems. Press.

19 To make the carrier loops for the cord belt, catch three lengths of cotton at the marked points on the outside of the side seams. Blanket stitch the threads to cover, fastening the thread securely at the end. Run the cord through the carrier loops to the desired length. Knot the ends and fluff out the free strands.

The slippers

When making the tailor-tack markings on the soles, mark the centre back heel in a different colour to the other tacks, to ensure that the slipper tops are applied the correct way around.

SLIPPER TOPS

1 Pin, tack and stitch the curved seam down the top of each foot. Remove the tacking and press. Clip the curves, and press the seam open. Pin, tack and stitch the back heel seams. Press the seams open.

LINING TOPS

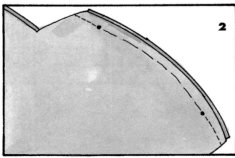

2 Pin and firmly tack the curved seam down the top of each foot. Starting at the top, stitch for 2.5cm (1in) then omit the machine stitching for the next 6.5cm (2½in). Machine stitch the remainder of the seam. Press, clip the curves and press the seams open.

3 Stitch the heel seams as for the slipper tops (see step 1).

ATTACHING THE SOLES

4 Work a double line of running stitches between the dots on the slipper and lining uppers. Attach the contrasting soles to the slipper tops, and the lining soles to the lining uppers. With right sides together and the slipper uppers facing, pin and tack the soles to the uppers, matching marks. Draw up the threads between tacks and ease the fullness smoothly around the toe area. Stitch; remove the tacking. Stitch again just inside the first line of stitching. Press the stitching only. Trim away excess fabric close to the stitching. Zigzag the raw edge of the seam and press, clipping the curves within the seam allowance.

ATTACHING THE LININGS TO THE SLIPPERS

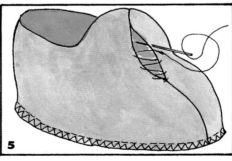

5 Undo the tacked area of the seam in front of the linings. With right sides together, pin, tack and stitch around the top edges of the slippers. Stitch again just inside the first line of stitching. Press and trim as before, clipping curves and angles. Turn the complete slipper right side out through the

untacked portion of the seamline in the lining. Slipstitch the edges of the opening together. Press the slipper edges and turn the slipper the correct way around.

SLIPPER TRIM

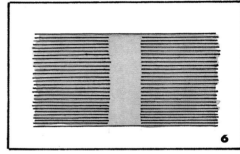

6 Cut a 5 x 4cm (2 x 1½in) rectangle of dressing-gown fabric for each slipper. Fringe each short end until only a 1.25cm (½in) strip of woven fabric remains in the centre.

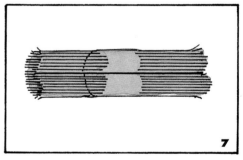

7 Turn the raw edges into the centre so they are encased; secure with a few stitches.

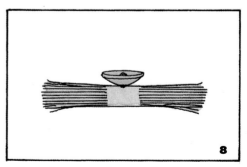

8 Sew a button to the top of each decoration. Sew the decoration to the centre front seam, 2.5cm (1in) away from the top of the slipper.

Lady's
BOUDOIR SET

The gown is made from a rich, softly patterned, pink and green printed acetate viscose brocade, with toning slipper-satin sleeves This is paired with a matching sleeveless nightgown in the same satin and accompanied by brocade slippers.

FABRIC REQUIREMENTS

FABRIC WIDTH	90cm (36in)	115cm (45in)	136cm (54in)	150cm (60in)
BOUDOIR GOWN AND SLIPPERS	1m (1yd)	50cm (½yd)	50cm (½yd)	50cm (½yd)
CONTRAST SLEEVES	25cm (10in)	25cm (10in)	25cm (10in)	25cm (10in)
BOUDOIR GOWN AND SLEEVES IN SINGLE FABRIC, PLUS SLIPPERS	1m (1yd)	70cm (¾yd)	70cm (¾yd)	70cm (¾yd)
NIGHTGOWN	50cm (½yd)	50cm (½yd)	50cm (½yd)	50cm (½yd)

TO FINISH

BOUDOIR GOWN AND SLIPPERS	Cord elastic • Small hook • 3mm (⅛in) wide ribbon: 2.3m (2½yd) in main colour, 1m (1yd) in contrast colour • 3 beads • Iron-on interfacing • Matching sewing thread
NIGHTGOWN	3mm (1/8in) wide ribbon: 90cm (1 yd) in main colour • 1m (1yd) fine-quality bias binding • Matching sewing thread

See page 91–93 for pattern templates

The boudoir gown

CUTTING OUT AND TRANSFERRING MARKINGS

Pin the pattern pieces onto the prepared fabric as directed on the pattern. Cut the pieces out. Transfer all markings from the pattern pieces to the fabric using tailor tacks and running tailor tacks.

FRONT AND BACK

1 With right sides together, join the two gown front sections to the gown back section at the shoulders. Stitch again just inside the first stitching. Trim the seam allowance close to the stitching and zigzag the edge. Press the seam flat and then towards the garment back.

FACINGS

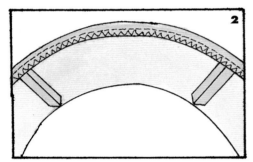

2 With right sides together, join the front facings to the back neck facing at the shoulders. Press the seams as stitched, and then press open. Zigzag around the entire outer edge of the joined facings. Turn under and press 6mm (¼in) along the same outer edge. Tack and stitch along this turning. Remove the tacking and press.

3 With right sides together, pin and tack the facing to the garment at the neck and front opening edges, matching the shoulder seams and centre backs. Stitch. On fabric that frays easily, stitch again just inside the first stitching, trim the seam allowance close to the stitching and zigzag the edge; clip and notch the curves, and press the seam away from the garment. On non-fraying fabric, clip and notch the single-stitched seam and press open. Turn the entire facing to the wrong side of the garment. Easing out the seamline to make a sharp edge, press and tack the facing into place, stopping about 13cm (5in) short of the lower edge of each front section.

SLEEVES

4 Turn under and tack a 6mm (¼in) hem along the lower edge of each sleeve. Press.

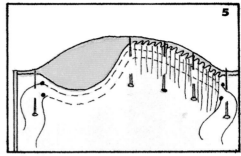

5 Make two parallel lines of running stitches between the dots on the sleeve heading, following the heading curve. With right sides together, pin the sleeve to the armhole opening at the dots. Draw up the threads of the running stitches between the pins. Distribute the gathers evenly, and pin

and tack into position. Stitch 1cm (⅜in) in from the edge. Stitch again just inside the first stitching. Trim the seam allowance close to the stitching, and zigzag the edge. Remove any tacking and gathering lying beyond the seam allowance. Press the stitching only, and then press the whole seam (still only at the stitching) towards the sleeve. Do *not* notch or clip the curves. Repeat steps 4 and 5 for the second sleeve.

SLEEVE AND SIDE SEAMS

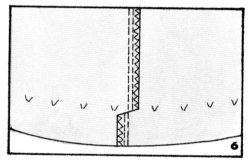

6 With right sides together and matching the hemlines and underarm seams, pin and tack each side and sleeve seam. Stitch a double row of stitching followed by zigzag, as before (step 1). Notch the allowance at the hemline angle, and clip the allowance at the sleeve foldline. Press the long seams to one side and the two short portions to the opposite side. This will reduce bulk in the finished hems.

SLEEVE HEMS AND GATHERED CUFF

7 Turn the lower sleeve edge up to the wrong side at the foldline, and tack the edge where it falls on the stitching line. Make a parallel line of tacking around the sleeve 1.25cm (½in) beneath the first. This double tacking will help prevent the fabric from 'walking' beneath the machine foot in the next step.

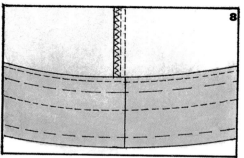

8 Machine stitch through all the layers 1.5mm (1⁄16in) from the sleeve upper edge, leaving an unstitched gap of 2.5cm (1in). Make a parallel line of stitching 6mm (¼in) away from the first, overlapping the end of the stitching onto the beginning stitches to make a continuous line. Remove all tacking and markings. Press. With a bodkin, insert cord elastic through the gap left in the casing, adjust and secure the elastic for a comfortable fit. Close the gap in the casing, using hand-sewn running stitches to continue the machine line. This allows for easy unpicking should the elastic need replacing over the years.

LOWER HEM AND FASTENING

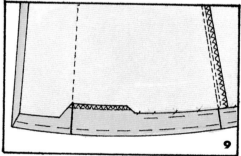

9 Machine stitch a line 6mm (¼in) from the lower hem edge. Trim away 3mm (⅛in) and zigzag the raw edge. Turn the hem up along the hemline marking, matching centres and side seams. Tack very close to the lower edge. Press, 'shrinking' the fabric to fit the garment. Cut away 1.25cm (½in) from the hem of the facings only, and turn under the zigzagged garment hem, to just cover the machine stitching. Tack again and then hem to the garment. Remove all tacking and

markings, and press. Turn the facings back to the wrong side and slipstitch the bottom and side edges to the finished hem. Catch the shoulder facings to the garment at the shoulder seams. Remove tacking and press.

10 Attach a hook to the right front, and a hand-stitched bar to the left front at the appropriate markings so that the gown closes edge-to-edge. Make a double bow with the ribbons and fasten with a single bead. Attach this to the right side of the right front, directly over the hook.

The slippers

CUTTING OUT AND TRANSFERRING MARKINGS

Pin the pattern pieces onto the prepared fabric as directed on the pattern. Cut the pieces out. Transfer all markings from the pattern pieces to the fabric using tailor tacks and running tailor tacks.

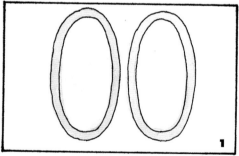

1 Draw around the sole pattern on iron-on interfacing. Cut out the shape 6mm (¼in) inside the drawn line. Iron the interfacing onto the wrong side of one pair of soles.

2 Working from dot to dot, make a line of machine stitching 6mm (¼in) away from the edges of all four sole sections, at the heel ends of the soles only. Notch the seam allowance around the stitched curves.

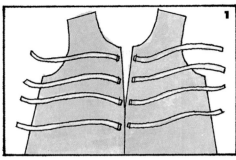

From this point, stitch just inside the first stitching. Trim the seam allowance close to the stitching and zigzag the edge. Press the seam flat and then to one side. Press the remaining 2cm (¾in) upper portion open. Turn the nightgown front to the right side. Cut eight 11cm (4¼in) lengths of matching ribbon and tack four to the front opening edges of each side at the marked dots.

FACING

2 With right sides together, join the front facing sections together from the dot to the bottom. Press the seam flat and then press it open. Turn under a 6mm (¼in) hem around the longest sides and across the bottom. Stitch and press.

ATTACHING FACING

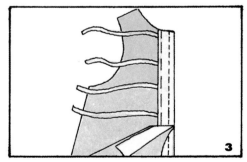

3 With right sides together and working one side at a time, match the remaining raw edges of the facing to the front opening. Pin, tack and stitch. Press the seam allowances away from the garment and remove the tacking. Also remove the tacking on the ribbons. Keeping the ribbons free, turn the facings back to the wrong side of the garment, tack and hem in position. Remove tacking and press.

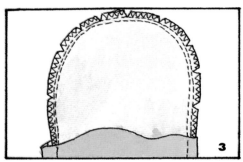

3 Make two parallel lines of running stitches along the long outer curve of the slipper tops. With right sides together, match the tops to the interfaced soles at the dots. Draw up the threads of the running stitches between the pins. Distribute the fabric around the curve so that there is greater fullness in the toe area than on the long sides. Tack and stitch. Stitch again just inside the first stitching. Trim the seam allowance close to the stitching, and zigzag the edge. Notch the curves. With the tip of the iron, press the stitching only. Remove any running stitches that are outside the seamline. Repeat for the slipper linings.

ATTACHING THE LININGS

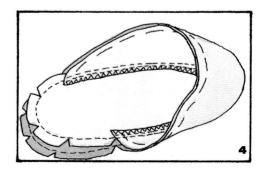

4 With the slipper wrong side out, and the lining right side out, slip the lining inside the slipper so that the right sides are together. Pin and tack around the remaining raw edges, matching the seams at the sides of the soles, but leaving the heels unjoined. Clip and press the seams open.

5 Turn the entire slipper right side out through the gap at the heel. Easing out the seamline, match the slipper to the lining, to form one neat shape. Turn in the raw edges of the heels and slipstitch the lining to the sole, just obscuring the stitched lines. Press. Repeat steps 4 and 5 for the second slipper. Attach double bows and a bead to each slipper front.

The nightgown

CUTTING OUT AND TRANSFERRING MARKINGS

Pin the pattern pieces onto the prepared fabric as directed on the pattern. Cut the pieces out. Transfer all markings from the pattern pieces to the fabric using tailor tacks and running tailor tacks.

FRONT

1 With right sides together, pin, tack and stitch the two front sections together at the centre, between the lowest dot and the hemline. Press the seam and clip the seam allowance 2cm (¾in) beneath the lower dot.

SHOULDERS AND NECK

4 With right sides together, join the front to the back section at the shoulders. Stitch again close to the first stitching. Trim the seam allowance close to the stitching and zigzag the edge. Press the seam flat and then press it towards the garment back.

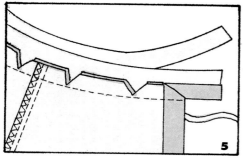

5 Turn the garment right side out. Open out one edge of bias binding. Leaving a little extra at the opening edge, match the bias edge to the entire neckline edge, finishing with a little extra at the opposite edge too. Press the stitching and press the bias strip away from the garment. Open out the other folded edge of the binding, and cut away 6mm (¼in) from the entire length, cutting along the fold line. Clip and notch the neckline edge.

6 Fold the entire bias binding over to the wrong side of the garment and tuck the new raw edge of the binding underneath to form a hem. Tack the entire neckline down, turning in the ends at the front opening. Hem the binding to the garment. Remove tacking and press.

SIDE SEAMS AND ARMHOLES

7 With right sides together, join the front to the back at the side seams using the usual method of double stitching followed by zigzagging. Press the seams towards the back of the garment and notch them at the hemline markings.

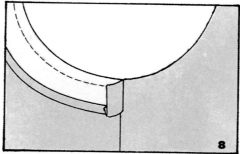

8 With the garment right side out, apply bias binding to the armholes as for the neckline (step 5). Remember to fold back the end of the binding at the underarm seam, so that the finished end will overlap it and the raw edge be covered up. Having sewn the bias into position, treat the binding and the armhole raw edges in exactly the same way as for the neckline, remembering to clip the garment edges. Hem in place, remove tacking and press.

HEM

9 Machine stitch across the bottom of the hem, 3mm (⅛in) from the edge. With the garment wrong side out, turn the hem up at the hemline markings and tack very close to the curved edge. Press the edge, gently 'shrinking' the excess fabric to fit the garment. Turn the raw edge under to just cover up the stitching line. Tack the hem to the garment close to the turned edge, and hem in place. Remove the tacking and press.

Gentleman's
DUNGAREES AND SHIRT

The checked shirt is made from pure cotton with long sleeves buttoned at the cuffs, which may be rolled up. Over the shirt a comfortable pair of dungarees, with a hand-embroidered motif of acorns and oak leaves to the bib pocket, provides enough room to accommodate an after-supper waistline.

FABRIC REQUIREMENTS

FABRIC WIDTH	90cm (36in)	115cm (45in)	136cm (54in)	150cm (60in)
SHIRT	1m (1yd)	70cm (¾yd)	50cm (½yd)	50cm (½yd)
DUNGAREES	1m (1yd)	70cm (¾ yd)	50cm (½yd)	50cm (½yd)

TO FINISH

SHIRT	Lightweight iron-on interfacing • 7 buttons • Matching sewing thread
DUNGAREES	2 waistband hooks and bar eyes • 2 large hooks and eyes • 14cm (5½in) embroidery frame • Stranded embroidery thread in 4 colours • Sewing thread in orange and to match

See page 94–96 for pattern templates

The shirt

CUTTING OUT AND TRANSFERRING MARKINGS

Pin the pattern pieces onto the prepared fabric as directed on the pattern. Cut the pieces out. Transfer all markings from the pattern pieces to the fabric using tailor tacks and running tailor tacks.

SHIRT FRONTS AND FACINGS

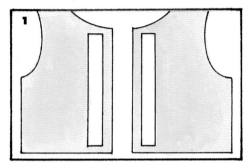

1 Using the front facing pattern, cut two strips of interfacing, trimming away the seam allowances. Iron a strip onto the wrong side of each shirt front.

2 Press under 6mm (¼in) along one edge of each front facing. Pin, tack, stitch and press.

3 With right sides together, match the facing raw edges to the shirt front edges. Pin, tack, stitch and then press the seams open. Trim the seam allowances and turn the facings back to the wrong sides of the garment. Tack down the facing edges as far as the bottom buttonhole marking.

BACK, YOKE AND SHOULDERS

4 Make two lines of gathering stitches between the dots around the curve of the shirt back.

5 Place the yoke and shirt back with right sides together, matching dots and centre backs. Draw up the gathering threads between the dots to fit. Pin, tack and stitch. Remove the tacking and gathers, then stitch

again just inside the first stitching. Trim close to stitching and zigzag raw edge to finish. Press the seam towards the yoke.

6 Join the fronts to the back at the shoulders, finishing the seams as in step 5. Press the seams towards the yoke.

COLLAR

7 Using the collar pattern as a guide, cut out one piece of interfacing, trimming away all seam allowances. Iron the interfacing onto the wrong side of one collar piece; this will be the undercollar.

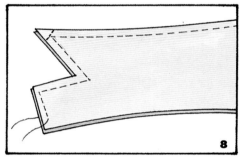

8 With right sides together, pin, tack and stitch the undercollar to the upper collar section, stopping 6mm (¼in) before the neck edge at each end. Stitch across the outer corners. Notch the curves and clip into the inner corners. Press the undercollar seam allowances back to the collar.

9 Turn up 6mm (¼in) along the neckline edge of the upper collar section. Tack and press. Turn the collar right side out, ease out the points and press.

JOINING COLLAR TO SHIRT

10 With right sides together, pin, tack and stitch the undercollar to the shirt at the neck edge, matching centre backs and matching dots to shoulder seams. Press. Notch the curves and press the seam open. Trim the seam allowances and press the entire seam back up towards the collar.

11 Fold down the tacked upper collar neckline edge, matching the centre back and shoulder marks to those on the neck edge. Slipstitch in place to just cover the neckline seam. Remove the tacking and press.

SLEEVES

12 Cut two 10 x 2.5cm (4 x 1in) strips of shirt fabric. On one long side of each strip, press under 6mm (¼in). Stitch a line 6mm (¼in) from the remaining long raw edge of each strip.

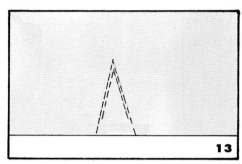

13 Using a small machine stitch, stitch along the marked lines at the sleeve hem. Pivot the needle at the point, reinforcing the point with extra stitches within the angle. Slash the fabric between the stitching, and spread the slash out to form a straight line.

14 With right sides together, pin, tack and stitch the unfolded edges of each strip to the slashed edge of each sleeve, matching the stitching lines. Remove the tacking and press flat.

15 Extend the binding and fold it back to the wrong side. Slipstitch the folded edge to the sewing line, encasing the raw edges of

the sleeve. Turn the front edge of the binding to the wrong side of the sleeve and tack in place.

16 Make a double line of running stitches between the dots on each sleeve head. With right sides together, pin the sleeve to the armhole opening, matching the back of the sleeve to the back of the garment and matching the dots. Draw up the gathers to fit. Tack and then stitch 2cm (¾in) from the edge. Stitch again just inside the first stitching. Repeat for the other sleeve. Trim the seams, press with the tip of the iron and zigzag around the raw edges.

17 Join the underarm and side seams in the usual way and finish the seams in the same way as for step 16.

18 Make two lines of gathering stitches along the lower edge of each sleeve.

CUFFS AND FINISHING

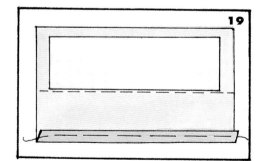

19 Using the cuff pattern section, cut a strip of interfacing to cover each cuff as far as the foldline. Iron the interfacing to the wrong side of the cuff section (the surface that will show the buttonhole stitching). Turn up, press and tack 6mm (¼in) on the uninterfaced side of the facing.

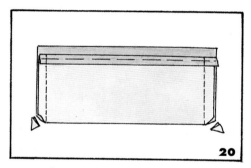

20 With right sides together, fold each cuff in half along the centre foldline. Stitch both side seams on each cuff. Trim the seams and corners; press. Turn the cuffs right out, ease out the corners and press flat.

21 With right sides together, position the end of the cuff that will have the button nearest the underarm seam. Align the buttonhole end of the cuff flush with the placket edge furthest away from the underarm seam. Draw up the threads and distribute the gathers evenly to fit the cuff. Tack and stitch. Remove the tacking, and press the seam to sink the stitches. Trim the seam allowances and pull the cuff down.

Press the seam allowances towards the cuff. Slipstitch the folded edge of the facing to the wrong side of the cuff, just covering the stitching lines.

22 Make hand or machine buttonholes at the positions marked. Press. Attach buttons where marked.

23 Turn up a 6mm (¼in) hem along the lower edge of the shirt; press. Trim 3mm (⅛in) away from the hem allowance across both of the facings.

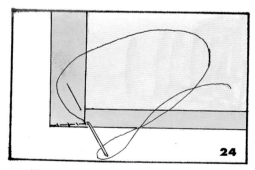

24 Turn up the same amount again along the lower edge and tack in place. Hem neatly to the shirt. Turn the facings back to the wrong side and slipstitch them to the hem and the bottom edge of the shirt. Remove all remaining tacking. Press.

The dungarees

CUTTING OUT AND TRANSFERRING MARKINGS

With the exception of the bib pocket, pin the pattern pieces onto the prepared fabric as directed on the pattern. Cut the pieces out. Transfer all markings from the pattern pieces to the fabric using tailor tacks and running tacks.

FRONT POCKETS AND DUNGAREE FRONTS

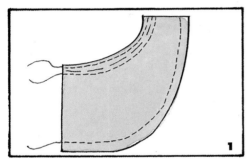

1 Zigzag stitch around both curved edges of each front pocket. Turn in a 6mm (¼in) hem around these edges, tack and press. Using orange thread and working from the right side, topstitch 3mm (⅛in) around all curved edges. On both short, curved edges only, stitch again 1.5mm (¹⁄₁₆in) in from the edge.

2 Join the dungaree front sections together down the centre and around the crotch, using matching thread. Stitch again just inside the first stitching. Trim the seam allowance close to the stitching, and zigzag the raw edges. Press. Press the seam to one side, notching the curve. Using orange thread and working from the right side, topstitch close to the seam. Press.

3 Matching dots, pin and tack the front pockets to the right side of the garment front. Using orange thread and working from the right side, join the pockets to the front, stitching 1.5mm (¹⁄₁₆in) from the

pocket edges. Leave the tacking in place and stitch close to the side seams, to hold. Press.

BACK POCKETS AND DUNGAREE BACKS

4 Zigzag stitch all around the two back pockets. Turn in a 6mm (¼in) hem around all edges and tack. Using orange thread, topstitch 3mm (⅛in) around all sides. Stitch again across the top of each pocket, 1.5mm (¹⁄₁₆in) from the edge.

5 Using orange thread, topstitch the two marked curve lines on each pocket. Press.

6 Join the dungaree back sections and finish as for step 2.

7 Pin and tack the back pockets to the dungaree back, matching dots. Using orange thread, stitch around the sides and bottom, 1.5mm (¹⁄₁₆in) from the edge. Remove the tacking and press.

BIB POCKET AND MOTIF

8 For ease of handling, the motif is applied to the fabric before the bib pocket is cut out. Fold a piece of denim with the grain running down, as before, so that the folded piece measures 10 x 18cm (4 x 7in).

9 Place the top bib pocket pattern on the fold as shown on the pattern. Pin, transfer markings then tailor tack completely around the pattern piece. Open out the fabric, clipping the tailor tacks between the layers. The tailor tacks indicate the eventual cutting line.

10 Trace the motif onto paper to make a template, cut out and place centrally between the marks on the opened-out bib pocket.

11 Set your design into the embroidery frame. Using a single strand of embroidery thread in the leaf colour, mark the outline of

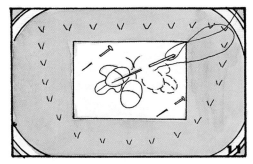

the template with running stitches around the outside. Also mark the remaining lines within the template with running stitches. Tear the paper template away. The puncture holes made by your needle will act as perforation lines.

12 Pad stitch each element using two strands of matching embroidery thread. Now, using a single strand, satin stitch to cover the padding. Finally, use two strands of thread to complete the leaf veins and stalks in outline stitch. Remove from the frame. Press from the back.

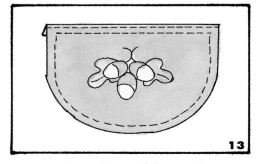

13 Cut the pocket out following the marked lines, and proceed as for step 8. Remove the tacking and press.

FRONT BIB AND WAISTBAND

14 Zigzag stitch around the raw edges of the bib. Turn in 6mm (¼in) around the sides and top. Pin, tack and press. Using orange thread and working from the right side, topstitch 3mm (⅛in) from the edge. Press. Make a second line of topstitching 1.5 mm (¹⁄₁₆ in) away from the edge.

15 Matching the bib pocket to the bib markings, pin, tack and stitch in orange around the sides and bottom, 1.5mm (¹⁄₁₆in) from the edge. Remove the tacking and tailor tacks from the pocket area only. Press.

16 With the wrong side of the dungarees facing, and matching the centres, pin and tack the bib to the garment so that the wrong side of the bib faces the wrong side of the dungarees. Place the front waistband in position at the waistline, with the wrong side facing up. Pin and tack. Using matching thread, stitch 1cm (⅜in) from the raw edges, stopping 6mm (¼in) before each end. Stitch again just inside the first stitching. Trim the seam allowance close to the stitching, and zigzag the raw edges. Press. Press the entire seam downwards towards the trouser section.

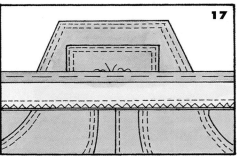

17 Tack up a 6mm (¼in) hem along the remaining long raw edge of the waistband. Press.

BACK BIB, STRAPS AND WAISTBAND

18 Zigzag around the raw edges of the back bib section and treat it in exactly the same way as for the front bib, step 14.

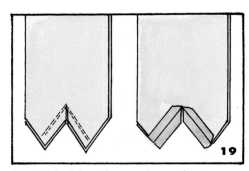

19 With right sides together and using matching thread, stitch the two strap pieces together around the central inward notch shape. Reinforce the point area of the notch. Clip into the point. Press, and then press the seam open. Trim the seam allowance.

20 Pin, tack and press a 6mm (¼in) hem to the wrong side of each long raw edge of both straps, and do the same across the ends.

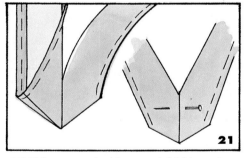

21 Take one tacked hem and fold it to the tacked hem on the same strip. Pin and tack the two hems together. Repeat the procedure for the second strap. Make sure that the centre seam at the join lies flat on itself. Tack across the bottom 1.25cm (½in) down from the central junction point.

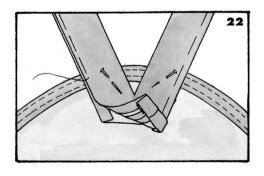

22 With the right side facing, place the back bib over the straps at the curved markings. Pin into position. Turn the bib to the wrong side, ensuring that the centre back of the straps falls over the centre of the bib. Lift the top surface of the strap base. Cut away 1.25cm (½in) of the under-surface of the strap and fold the top surface back down and the raw edge under. Tack in place. Tack inside the edges of the straps.

23 Using orange thread, working from the wrong side of the bib, and starting across the bottom of the strap, stitch the strap to the bib 1.5mm (¹⁄₁₆in) from the edge. Continue stitching around all edges of both straps and back into the bib. Remove all tacking from the straps except the tailor tacks at the strap ends. Press.

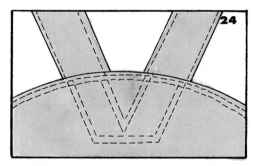

24 Using orange thread and working from the right side of the bib, stitch again just inside the new line, working the curved portions into the existing stitching. Secure the ends and press.

25 Attach the back bib and waistband to the dungaree back in exactly the same way as for the front, steps 16 and 17.

SIDE SEAMS

26 On the front and back garment sections, zigzag stitch the raw edges from waist to notch. Press.

27 With right sides together, pin and tack the side seams together, omitting the waistbands but matching the waistband

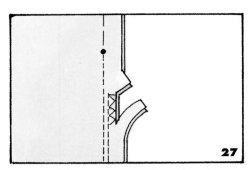

seam and dots. Using matching thread, stitch from the side dots to the dungaree hems. Clip to the seamline just under the outward-facing notches. Remove the tacking from the stitched area only. Stitch again just inside the first stitching, and finish seams.

28 Press open the remaining tacked portion of the side seams and tack to the garment.

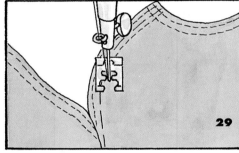

29 Keeping the garment turned inside out, and with the right side of the garment facing upwards under the presser foot, make a double line of orange topstitching around the tacked opening in the usual manner.

30 Remove all tacking including the tacking which is holding the seam edges together. Press.

WAISTBANDS AND INSIDE LEG SEAM

31 On both the front and back waistbands, with the right side of the garment facing, pin the waistband down onto the garment, turning in each end. Tack and topstitch 1.5mm (¹⁄₁₆in) from the edge around all waistband edges. Remove the tacking; press

32 Zigzag across the bottom raw edges of the legs. With right sides together, join the inside leg seam, carefully matching the centre crotch. Stitch again just inside the first stitching and finish the raw edges in the usual manner. Press.

HEMS AND FINISHING
33 Tack up a 6mm (¼in) hem to the wrong side of the dungarees. Turn the hem up again along the hem marking lines. Using orange thread, make a double line of machine stitching along the hem in the usual way.

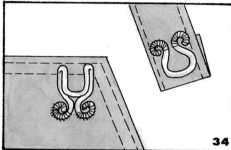

34 Attach large metal hook fasteners to the marks on the bib front. Fix the eye sections to the upper markings on the strap ends. Turn the straps back at the lower markings and secure firmly to the strap undersides.

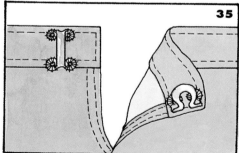

35 Attach a hook at either end of the front waistband and a bar at either end of the back waistband so that the front overlaps the back by 2.5cm (1in), according to the markings. Trim any loose threads and remove any remaining markings. Press.

Lady's
PARTY OUTFIT

The party dress is made of 100 per cent pure cotton. Its double-circle ruffle skirt sits neatly around the waist and bursts into wonderful spinning fullness around the hemline, which is bound in a contrasting colour. The tie fastening of the halter neckline gives way to a back that is bare almost to the waist. The bodice fastens with a simple button fastening. Underneath the dress, a fine white cotton lawn petticoat exactly echoes the dress and is bound in the same contrasting colour. Beneath the petticoat are knickers to match the dress.

FABRIC REQUIREMENTS

FABRIC WIDTH	90cm (36in)	115cm (45in)	136cm (54in)	150cm (60in)
DRESS AND KNICKERS	70cm (¾yd)	50cm (½yd)	50cm (½yd)	50cm (½yd)
PETTICOAT	50cm (½yd)	50cm (½yd)	50cm (½yd)	50cm (½yd)

TO FINISH

DRESS AND PETTICOAT	Matching sewing thread • 70cm (¾yd) matching ribbon, 3mm (⅛in) wide • 4.4m (4¾yd) contrasting bias binding • 1 matching button • hook and bar, size 0
KNICKERS	Matching sewing thread • 50cm (½yd) elastic, 6mm (¼in) wide

See page 97–99 for pattern templates

The party dress

CUTTING OUT AND TRANSFERRING MARKINGS

Pin the pattern pieces onto the prepared fabric as directed on the pattern. Cut the pieces out. Transfer all markings from the pattern pieces to the fabric using tailor tacks and running tailor tacks.

BODICE

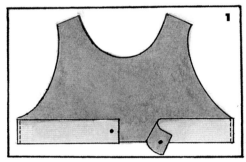

1 With right sides together, join the front bodice section to the back bodice sections at the side seams (using the short unmarked edges of the back sections). Press the seams flat and then press them open. Repeat this process for the bodice lining. Trim away 3mm (⅛in) of fabric from the lining seam allowances. Press under a 6mm (¼in) hem on the waistline edge of the lining.

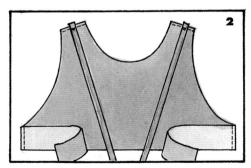

2 With the lining right side up, and raw edges even, tack a 25cm (10in) length of ribbon to each shoulder edge. Stitch 3mm (⅛in) away from the edge. Press.

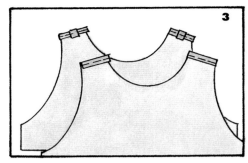

3 Press under 6mm (¼in) to the shoulder edges of both front bodice pieces. Tack.

4 With right sides together, pin, tack and stitch the bodice to the lining, matching the side seams and armhole edges. Stitch around the neckline, around the armhole edges, across the top of the back bodice and down the back opening, stopping 6mm (¼in) from the waistline edge. Leave the shoulder seams open. Take care to keep the ribbon ties on the inside of the garment and free from the seamlines. Stitch diagonally across the back bodice corners. Remove the tacking.

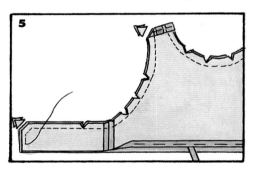

5 Press the seams flat, notch the neckline curve and clip and notch the armhole curves. Trim the seam allowances diagonally across the corners. Press the seams open, and taper the seam allowances close to the stitching at the shoulder edges. Turn the bodice right side out and gently ease out the corners and the shoulders. Press.

THE SKIRT SECTIONS

6 Zigzag all the straight edges of the skirt sections. With right sides together, join the two skirt sections at the centre front, taking a 6mm (¼in) seam. Press the seam flat and then press it open.

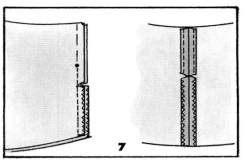

7 Pin and tack the centre back seam, matching the dots and using them as a guide for the 1cm (⅜in) seam allowance. Starting from the dot 5cm (2in) below the waistline edge, machine stitch the seam. Clip the seam allowance 2.5cm (1in) below the seam opening. Remove the tacking from the machine-stitched portion only. Press the entire seam flat. Turn under 3mm (⅛in) along the back opening seam allowances as far as the clip. Tack, stitch and press. Tack the seam allowances back to the skirt at the waistline edge. Trim 3mm (⅛in) off the seam allowances of the lower portion of the back seam. Zigzag stitch the new raw edges. Remove the remaining tacking from the centre back seam.

JOINING THE SKIRT TO THE BODICE

8 Make two parallel lines of running stitches 3mm (⅛in) and 1cm (⅜in) away from the waistline edge of the skirt.

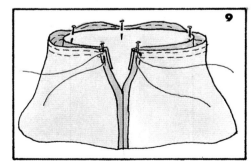

9 With right sides together, match and pin the skirt centre front to the bodice centre front, and the skirt back opening to the bodice back opening.

11 Open out one folded edge of bias binding, and turn under 1cm (⅜in) at one end. With right sides together, align the folded end of the binding with the centre back seam. Matching the raw edges, pin the binding to the entire garment hem, allowing the second end of the binding to overlap the folded end by 1cm (⅜in). Stitch along the binding foldline. Press the seam towards the hem edge. Turn the garment wrong side out and turn the folded edge of the binding down so that it peeps beyond the raw hem edge. Slipstitch the folded binding edge to the hem seamline. Press.

12 With the garment right side out, make a hand- or machine-stitched buttonhole on the left bodice section at the marked point. Sew the button on at the corresponding mark on the right bodice section. Press the entire dress.

The matching knickers

CUTTING OUT AND TRANSFERRING MARKINGS

Pin the pattern pieces onto the prepared fabric as directed on the pattern. Cut the pieces out. Transfer all markings from the pattern pieces to the fabric using tailor tacks and running tailor tacks.

1 With right sides together, stitch the back and front knicker sections together at the crotch. Make a second line of stitching close to the first within the seam allowance. Press and trim close to the stitching. Zigzag the raw edge and press. Press the entire seam to one side.

2 Join both side seams in exactly the same way. Press to one side.

10 Draw up the running stitches and distribute the gathers evenly around the waistline. Pin, tack and stitch. Press the seam open and then press it flat towards the bodice. Stitch again just inside the first stitching. Trim close to the stitching and zigzag the raw edge. Press the seam allowance up towards the bodice. Remove the lower line of running stitches from the skirt gathers. Turn the garment inside out and slipstitch the bodice lining into place at the waistline. Press.

HEM AND BACK FASTENING

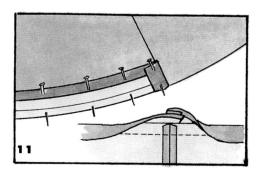

11

3 Press under 6mm (¼in) across the entire waistline edge. Fold over again along the marked foldline. Tack in place. Machine stitch the heading to the garment, close to the tacked edge, starting 5cm (2in) away from a side seam and finishing 2.5cm (1in) short of the starting point.

4 With a bodkin or a safety pin, insert a length of elastic through the heading so that when the elastic is stitched it measures 33cm (13in) around. Flip the unstitched edge of the heading over to cover the elastic, and secure the heading to the garment by hand.

5 Bind the two leg holes with the bias binding in exactly the same way as for the dress hem (step 11), starting and finishing at the crotch. Press.

The contrasting petticoat

CUTTING OUT AND TRANSFERRING MARKINGS

Use the skirt pattern pieces from the party dress, pinning them onto the prepared fabric as directed on the pattern. Cut the pieces out. Transfer all markings from the pattern pieces to the fabric using tailor tacks and running tailor tacks.

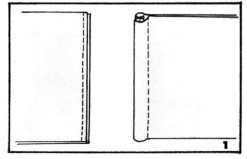

1 The two petticoat sections are sewn together at the front with a French seam. With wrong sides together, stitch 1–2mm (¹⁄₁₆in) away from the raw edges. Press. Open the two sections out and press the seam to one side. Then, with right sides together,

tack the same seam, encasing the raw edges. Check that none of the raw edges show, and stitch. Remove the tacking. Press.

2 With right sides together, tack and stitch the remaining seam at the centre back, beginning the machine stitching from the second dot below the waistline edge. Remove the tacking from the machine-stitched portion only. Press the seam flat and then press the entire seam open. Press

under 3mm (¹⁄₈in) on each seam allowance. Tack and stitch each seam allowance to the garment close to the edges. Remove the remaining tacking and press.

3 Make two lines of running stitches around the waistline 3mm (¹⁄₈in) and 1cm (³⁄₈in) from the edge. Fold the waistband in half lengthwise and press. Press under a 6mm (¼in) hem along one long raw edge, and tack in place.

4 With right sides together, and matching the centre dot to the centre, and the back opening dots to the back opening edges, pin the garment to the waistband at these points. Draw up the threads of the running stitches between the pins and distribute the gathers evenly along the waistband. Pin, tack and stitch 6mm (¼in) away from the waistline edge.

5 Press the seam open and then press it back up again towards the waistband. Stitch again just inside the first stitching. Trim close to the stitching and zigzag the raw edge. Press.

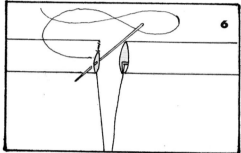

6 Turn in the 6mm (¼in) seam allowances at each end of the waistband. Press, and fold the waistband over towards the wrong side of the garment. Slipstitch the edge to the seamline, and slipstitch the open ends of each end of the waistband.

7 Turn the garment right side out and sew a hook and bar eye at the marked points so that the left side overlaps and hooks into the bar on the other side. Attach bias binding to the hem edge and finish in exactly the same way as for the dress (step 11). Press.

Gentleman's PYJAMAS

The pyjamas are made in a quietly dashing rich crimson polyester taffeta with black velvety spots. The pyjama top is trimmed at the sleeves and pocket with black braid, and the pyjama trouser cord is also black. The bottoms are cut with as few seams as possible, for ease and comfort of wear.

FABRIC REQUIREMENTS

FABRIC WIDTH	90cm (36in)	115cm (45in)	136cm (54in)	150cm (60in)
PYJAMAS	1.2m (1¼yd)	1.2m (1¼yd)	1m (1yd)	70cm (¾yd)

TO FINISH

PYJAMAS	70cm (¾yd) ornamental braid • 3 buttons • Small piece of iron-on interfacing • 1.2m (1¼yd) cord • Matching sewing thread

See page 100–101 for pattern templates

The pyjama jacket

CUTTING OUT AND TRANSFERRING MARKINGS

Pin the pattern pieces onto the prepared fabric as directed on the pattern. Cut the pieces out. Transfer all markings from the pattern pieces to the fabric using tailor tacks and running tailor tacks.

FRONT POCKET, SHOULDER SEAMS AND FACINGS

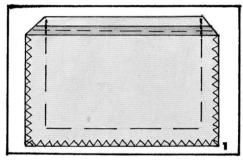

1 Turn under 6mm (¼in) on the top edge of the pocket. Tack and press. Fold the pocket top over to the right side along the foldline. Tack in place at the side edges. Zigzag around the pocket sides and bottom. Stitch the flap to the pocket as tacked. Press. Clip the corners diagonally. Turn the flap to the wrong side, gently ease out the corners of the pocket and then slipstitch the hem in place. Press.

2 Turn under 6mm (¼in) on all remaining raw edges. Tack and press. Hand sew braid to the right side of the pocket top, positioning it so that it is directly above the hemline (which is on the wrong side). Secure the braid ends firmly to the wrong side. Press. Place the pocket on the right side of the pyjama front so that the pocket is on the left breast of the garment, matching dots. Tack and hand sew. Remove the tacking and press.

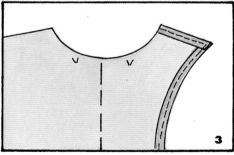

3 Turn under, tack and press a 6mm (¼in) hem on the long, curved edge of each facing section, and again across the shoulder facing. Stitch close to the edges. Remove the tacking and press.

4 With right sides together, join the fronts to the back at the shoulder seams. Stitch again just inside the first stitching. Trim the seam allowances close to the stitching and zigzag the raw edges. Press the seams towards the back of the garment.

COLLAR AND FACINGS

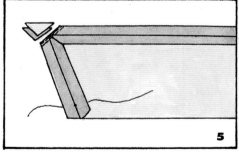

5 With right sides together, join the two collar pieces, leaving the neck edge open and stopping the seams 6mm (¼in) short of the neck edge at each side. Using very small machine stitches, sew across the collar points to blunt them slightly. Press the seam allowances open, and trim diagonally across the collar points. Trim the seam allowances and turn the collar right side out, easing out the points. Press.

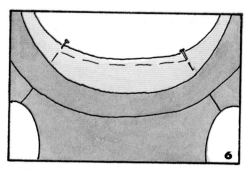

6 With right sides together and matching the centres and the shoulder dots to the shoulders, pin and tack a single thickness of the collar to the garment at the neck edge between the shoulder seams.

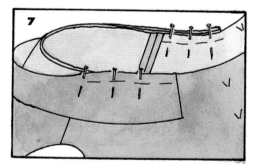

7 Pin both layers of the collar to the garment, from the shoulder seams to the collar ends at the front of the garment.

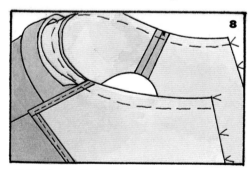

8 Fold each facing back on itself along the foldline so that the right side of the facing is against the right side of the garment, matching the facing neckline dots to the garment neckline. Tack in place. Clip the upper collar section to the seamline at the shoulder seams.

9 Tack the entire neckline, omitting the upper collar section (a single thickness)

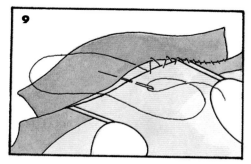

between the shoulders. Machine stitch. Press as stitched and notch the curves. Press the entire seam open. Now press the front neckline seam completely downwards and press the entire neckline seam between the shoulders up towards the collar. Turn the facings right side out, easing out the front corners. Turn under a 6mm (¼in) hem on the raw edge of the collar as marked, and slipstitch to the garment neckline seam. Slipstitch the facings to the shoulders at the shoulder seams.

SLEEVES AND SIDE SEAMS

10 Make two lines of running stitches between the tailor tacks on the sleeve head. With right sides together, match the sleeve tailor tacks to the armhole tailor tacks. Draw up the running stitches to ease the fabric into the armhole section. Tack. Machine stitch 1cm (⅜in) from the armhole edges. Stitch again just inside the first stitching. Trim the seam allowances close to the stitching. Zigzag the raw edges. Press the stitching only.

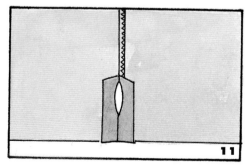

11 With right sides together, join the side and sleeve seams matching the underarm seam; stop the stitching at the marked dot

on the sleeve seam and resume the seam again at the lower dot. This gap in the seam will allow you to tuck the braid trim inside the seamline, concealing and protecting the raw ends. Clip the seam allowance at the upper end of the gap, and press open the lower portion of the seam allowances, including the gap. Finish the upper arm portion of the sleeve and the side seams in the usual way (see page 10). To reduce bulk at the hem edge, make notches in the seam allowances of the garment hemline. Press under 6mm (¼in) on the sleeve hems, and turn under again along the marked hemline. Hem in place and press lightly.

HEMS AND FINISHING

12 With the garment wrong side out, open out the facings and cut 6mm (¼in) off the bottom of the facings only. Turn up a 6mm (¼in) hem along the remainder of the hem edge, and tack. Turn the hem up again along the marked hemline and stitch. Return the facings to their correct positions on the inside of the garment, and slipstitch the bottom and side edges to the garment hem. Press.

13 Slip the end of the braid into the gap provided at the underarm sleeve seam. Hand sew the braid to the right side of the garment sleeves, so that it lies along the hand-stitched hem (which is on the wrong side). Slip the finishing end of the braid into the seamline and secure, closing up the gap if necessary.

14 Make buttonholes by hand or machine on the pocket side of the garment front at the buttonhole markings. Sew buttons onto the opposite front to correspond with the buttonholes. Press the garment lightly and remove any remaining threads or tacking.

The pyjama bottoms

CUTTING OUT AND TRANSFERRING MARKINGS

Pin the pattern pieces onto the prepared fabric as directed on the pattern. Cut the pieces out. Transfer all markings from the pattern pieces to the fabric using tailor tacks and running tailor tacks.

CORD EXIT AND FRONT AND BACK SEAMS

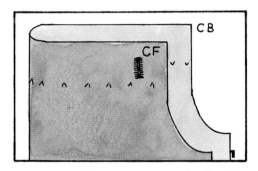

1 Open out the trouser section that has the cord exit marking. Press a small piece of iron-on interfacing directly over the exit mark on the wrong side. Working from the right side, make a buttonhole at the marked exit point. Press. This exit buttonhole will fall at the centre front of the garment.

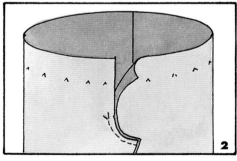

2 With right sides together, stitch the entire length of the curved centre back seam. Stitch again just inside the first stitching. Trim the seam allowances close to the stitching. Zigzag the raw edge. Press, and notch the curve. Keeping the right sides together, join the centre front seam in the same way, but stitching only from the marked dot (part way down the seam) down and around the curve. Clip the seam allowance at the dot. Notch the curved seam allowance and press to one side.

FRONT OPENING AND WAISTLINE HEADING

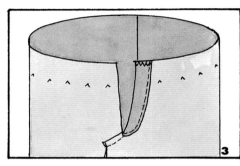

3 You will be using one facing section as cut, and the second facing section as only a single thickness. On a single thickness of facing, turn under a 6mm (¼in) hem. Tack and press. With right sides together, and matching the dot at the base of the curve to the dot at the front seam of the garment, tack and sew the facing to the garment. Press the seam open, and then press the entire seam away from the garment. Fold the facing back at the seamline to the wrong side of the garment. Tack in place. Working from the wrong side of the garment, machine stitch the facing to the garment close to the facing edge. Remove the tacking and zigzag the faced area together at the waistline edge. Press.

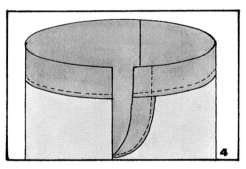

4 Turn the garment wrong side out. Turn under and tack a 6mm (¼in) hem along the entire waistline edge. Turn under again to the marked stitching line. Tack the hem to the garment. Machine stitch through all thicknesses close to the tacked edge. Remove the tacking and press.

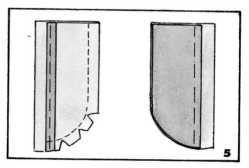

5 Place the two pieces of the remaining facing section with right sides together. Stitch around the curved edge, stopping at the marked dot. Turn a 6mm (¼in) hem to the wrong side on a single thickness of the facing. Tack. Notch the curved seam allowance and press open. Trim the seam allowance. Turn right side out and press.

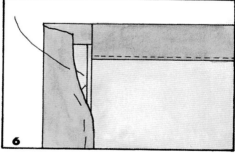

6 Place the long raw edge of the facing to the remaining raw edge of the garment, matching the dots at the seamline opening. Tack and sew. Remove the tacking and press the seam open, then press the entire seam away from the garment. Turn the garment wrong side out. Turn the top of the facing down in line with the waistband top edge. Trim the excess fabric away and tack the facing edge to the garment so that it just covers the seamline down the front opening.

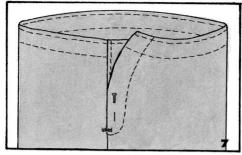

7 Turn the garment right side out and machine stitch the facing close to the front seamline. Make a line of machine stitching along the entire length of the waistband, close to the top edge. Press.

Pin the front opening over the facing extension. Make a bar tack at the base of the opening.

INSIDE LEG SEAM, HEMS AND FINISHING

8 With right sides together, join the inside leg seam, matching the centre crotch. Stitch again just inside the first stitching, and trim close to the stitching. Zigzag the raw edge. Clip the seam at the hemline, and notch the curves. Press the seam to one side.

9 Turn under 6mm (¼in) on the lower edge of each leg; press. Turn under again along the marked hemline, and sew the hem to the garment. Remove the tacking and press.

10 Attach the drawstring to a bodkin or safety pin and thread it through the waistline heading, leaving enough at either end to tie around your gentleman's waist.

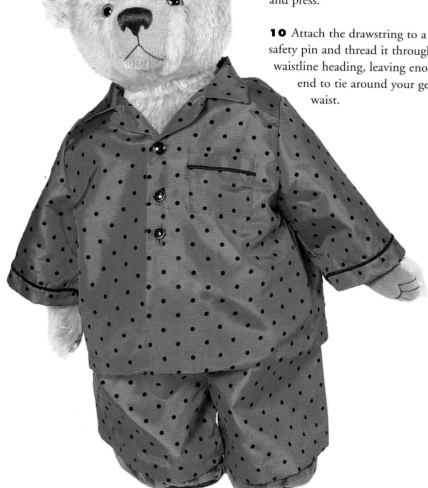

Lady's COAT

Made from a fabric of mixed silk, wool and linen fibres, the lined coat is styled to look elegant while still being capable of covering large party skirts or extra woollies. The collarless neckline fastens snugly under the chin and neatly down the front with four buttons. The skirt flares from a gently curved bodice at the front and a deeply inverted V-shape at the back bodice.

FABRIC REQUIREMENTS

FABRIC WIDTH	90cm (36in)	115cm (45in)	136cm (54in)	150cm (60in)
COAT	70cm (¾yd)	50cm (½yd)	50cm (½yd)	50cm (½yd)
LINING	50cm (½yd)	50cm (½yd)	50cm (½yd)	50cm (½yd)

TO FINISH

COAT	Iron-on interfacing • 4 buttons • Matching sewing thread

See page 102–103 for pattern templates

The coat

CUTTING OUT AND TRANSFERRING MARKINGS

Pin the pattern pieces onto the prepared fabric as directed on the pattern. Cut the pieces out. Transfer all markings from the pattern pieces to the fabric using tailor tacks and running tailor tacks.

When cutting and marking the lining for the coat, note that the skirt portions of the lining use the same pattern pieces as those for the coat itself. For the lining, the front pattern is to be folded back out of the way, along the line labelled 'lining cutting line'. For the lining hemline, use the upper dotted hemlines on both the front and back skirt portions.

FRONT BODICE AND SKIRT

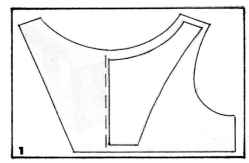

1 Using the bodice pattern as a guide, cut two pieces of iron-on interfacing to the shape shown above. Trim away 6mm (¼in) from the shoulder, neckline and waistline edges only. Iron one strip onto the wrong side of each bodice front, butting the edge up to the foldline.

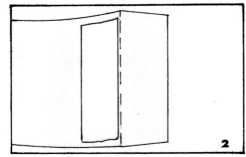

2 Cut two 4.5 x 16.5cm (1¾ x 6½in) strips of iron-on interfacing for the coat skirt fronts. Trim 1cm (⅜in) away from the waistline edge and 1.25cm (½in) from the hemline edge of each strip. Iron one strip onto the wrong side of each skirt front.

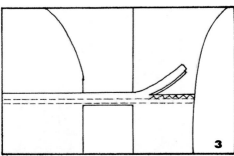

3 With right sides together, pin and tack the skirt sections to the bodice sections, matching the edges together and easing the skirt onto the bodice between the two dots. Stitch 1cm (⅜in) from the raw edge. Remove the tacking, and press the seams open with the tip of the iron only. Press the seam allowance again, up towards the bodice. Stitch again just inside the first stitching. Trim the fabric close to the stitching, and zigzag the seam edge. Clip and notch the curves and press the finished seam again towards the bodice.

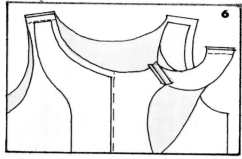

6 With right sides together, and making sure that the back neck facing joining the two front sections remains untwisted, pin, tack and stitch the front bodice to the back at the shoulders. Press the seam flat and then press it open. Trim the seam allowances as for step 4.

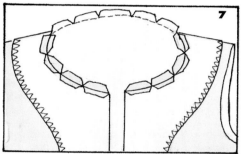

7 Turn the garment right side out and fold the facings back along the front foldlines, onto the right side of the garment. Matching the centre backs and shoulder seams, pin, tack and stitch around the neckline. Trim the seam allowances, clip and notch the curves and diagonally clip the front corner allowances. Press the seam open.

8 Turn the facings to the inside of the garment. Easing out the points and curves, press the facing around the neckline edge. Press the centre front openings along their foldlines. Tack the facings to the garment close to the sewn edges, stopping 5cm (2in) short of each front hemline marking.

BACK NECK AND FRONT FACING

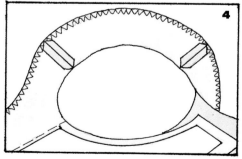

4 With right sides together, join the back neck facing to the front bodice facings at the shoulders. Press the seam flat and then open. Make diagonal cuts into the seam allowances as shown. Zigzag the entire outer edge of the joined facings.

BACK BODICE AND SKIRT

5 Make a line of machine stitching 6mm (¼in) from the skirt waistline edge, and do the same for the bodice waistline. Clip to the stitching at the centres. With right sides together, pin and tack the skirt to the back bodice, easing and manipulating the fabric to a smooth fit. Stitch 1cm (⅜in) away from the raw edges. Treat the seam in the same way as for the Front Skirt and Bodice (step 3). Make a notch at the centre back point.

SLEEVES

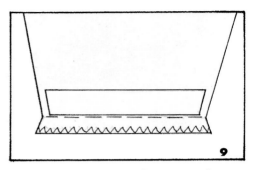

9 Cut two 2.5cm (1in) deep strips of iron-on interfacing. Butting the edge up to the hemline marking at the lower sleeve, and with the ends 6mm (¼in) short of each side edge, iron one strip into place on the wrong side of each sleeve. Zigzag the raw edges at the sleeve bottoms. Press.

10 Make two parallel lines of running stitches between the dots around the sleeve heads. With right sides together, and matching the sleeve dots to those of the garment armhole opening, pin one sleeve in place. Draw up the threads of the running stitches. Eliminating tucks and gathers, pin and tack the sleeve to fit smoothly into the armhole. Stitch 1cm (⅜in) from the raw edges. Remove the tacking and running stitches. Stitch again just inside the first stitching, and trim close to the stitching. Zigzag the edge. With the tip of the iron, press only the stitching. Still using only the iron tip, press the entire armhole seam towards the sleeve. Do *not* clip or notch any curves. Repeat for the other sleeve.

SIDE AND SLEEVE SEAMS

11 With right sides together and matching hemline markings, waistline and armhole seams, pin, tack and stitch each side seam, starting from the sleeve bottom. Press the seams flat and then open, notching the allowances at each hemline point.

HEMS AND FACINGS

12 Keeping the garment wrong side out, turn up and tack the lower sleeve edges at the hemline markings. Herringbone stitch them to the interfacing, taking care to prevent any stitching from showing on the right side of the garment. Press.

13 Make a line of machine stitching 3mm (⅛in) from the raw edge around the entire lower edge of the skirt, then zigzag the raw edge. With the garment wrong side out, turn the hem up at the marked hemline, easing any fullness into the allowance. Trim away a fraction of the zigzagged edge at the facing sections only. Tack the hem close to the lower edge, and again close to the zigzagged edge. Press. A good fabric should shrink very neatly to fit the hem. Now, ensuring that the stitching is invisible on the right side of the garment, herring-bone stitch the hem in place. Remove the tacking and press.

14 With the garment still wrong side out, match and catch the facings to the shoulder and waistline seams. Catch the front facings where they cross the hem itself, using herringbone stitch, and slipstitch the facing hem edges to the garment hem edge. Catch the facing edges to the garment interfacing for 4cm (1½in) above, and the same amount below, the skirt/bodice seam. Press.

FASTENINGS

15 Make four hand or machine-stitched buttonholes at the buttonhole markings, ensuring that the coat will fasten the ladies' way (right over left). Press. Sew the buttons to the corresponding markings on the opposite front.

MAKING THE LINING

16 Make the lining in exactly the same way as for the coat, steps 3, 5, 6, 10 and 11, and in the same sequence. Turn the sleeves up at the hemline markings, tack and press.

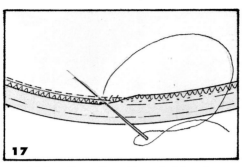

17 Make a line of machine stitching 6mm (¼in) from the lower edge of the lining. Trim 3mm (⅛in) away from the allowance and zigzag the raw edge. With the lining wrong side out, turn the hem up at the marked hemline. Pin, easing the fabric to fit the curves. Tack close to the hem edge and again just under the zigzagged edge. Press. Turn back the zigzagged hem edge with your thumb to expose the machine-stitched line. Catch the hem into place along the machine-stitched line. Remove the tacking and press.

18 Make a line of machine stitching 6mm (¼in) from the raw edge around the entire neckline and the front openings.

ATTACHING THE LINING

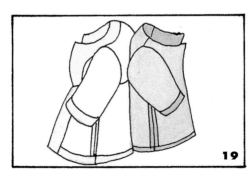

19 Turn both the coat and the lining wrong side out. Place the coat and lining back to back.

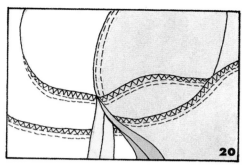

20 Matching the side and sleeve seams together, lay the opened seams directly over each other. Beginning at the underarm seam, pin and backstitch the sleeve seam allowance to the garment sleeve allowance. Make the join about 5cm (2in) long.

21 Inserting your hand in the sleeve lining via the front opening, grasp both lining and garment hems together, and pull the lining over the coat so that now the wrong sides of both are together.

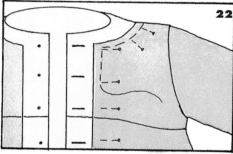

22 Matching the shoulder and front bodice seams, pin and tack the lining to the coat around the neckline and front opening edges, covering up the machine stitching and clipping the curves to the stitching where necessary. Slipstitch the lining to the coat and remove the tacking.

HEM FINISHING

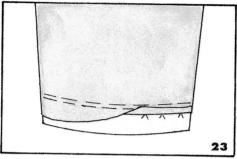

23 Tack the sleeve linings to the garment 1.25cm (½in) from the lining hem edges. Hem the linings to the sleeves 3mm (⅛in) under the hemline, so that the stitching is covered by a fold at the lower edge. Remove tacking.

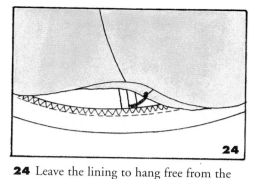

24 Leave the lining to hang free from the garment, except at the side seams, which are caught together by a French tack. To make the French tack, take a small stitch at the top of the garment hem, and another at the top of the lining hem, at the seamlines. Leave some slack between the two, and repeat at the same position. Secure the link with a backstitch, and then blanket stitch across the entire slack portion, to cover. Secure and finish the sewing thread.

Gentleman's
JACKET, WAISTCOAT AND BOW-TIE

The lined, pure wool, tweed jacket is designed for elegance as well as warmth. The pocket flaps are faced with lining fabric to reduce bulk and preserve a smooth line. Beneath the jacket the snug-fitting cotton poplin waistcoat has slashed pockets, and the whole is lined and backed with a paler shade of poplin. The poplin bow-tie fastens at the back of the neck with a press stud to avoid those awkward fumblings when tying a bow-tie from scratch.

FABRIC REQUIREMENTS

FABRIC WIDTH	90cm (36in)	115cm (45in)	136cm (54in)	150cm (60in)
JACKET	1m (1yd)	70cm (¾yd)	70cm (¾yd)	50cm (½yd)
JACKET LINING	1m (1yd)	70cm (¾yd)	70cm (¾yd)	70cm (¾yd)
WAISTCOAT	50cm (½yd)	50cm (½yd)	50cm (½yd)	50cm (½yd)
WAISTCOAT LINING	30cm (¼yd)	30cm (¼yd)	30cm (¼yd)	30cm (¼yd)
BOW-TIE	50cm (½yd)	50cm (½yd)	50cm (½yd)	50cm (½yd)

TO FINISH

JACKET	Lightweight iron-on interfacing • Matching sewing thread • 3 buttons
WAISTCOAT	Lightweight iron-on interfacing • Matching sewing thread • 5 buttons
BOW-TIE	Matching sewing thread • Press stud

See page 104–108 for pattern templates

The jacket

CUTTING OUT AND TRANSFERRING MARKINGS

Pin the pattern pieces onto the prepared fabric as directed on the pattern. Cut the pieces out. Transfer all markings from the pattern pieces to the fabric using tailor tacks and running tailor tacks.

POCKETS AND FRONTS

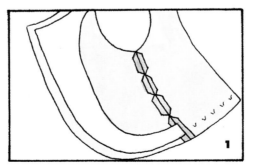

1 Using the front facing pattern, cut out two pieces of iron-on interfacing, trimming away the seam allowances from the shoulder, curved inner edge and side seam. Iron into place on the wrong side of each jacket front. With right sides together, pin and tack an underarm panel to each jacket front, easing

the fabric between the notches. Press to sink the stitches into the fabric. Notch the curves and press the seams open.

2 Apply interfacing to the wrong sides of the pocket flap facings. With right sides together, pin, tack and stitch a pocket flap to each pocket facing, making sure you remember to leave the straight edges open. Remove the tacking; press. Trim the seam and notch the curves. Turn right side out and press, easing the facing edge under the seamline very slightly. Stitch the raw edges together close to the top edge to hold the layers.

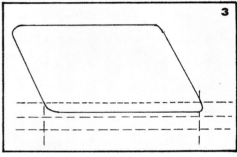

3 If the fabric is loosely woven or soft, press a 5 x 4cm (2 x 1½in) piece of interfacing over the pocket markings on the wrong side of each jacket front. On the right side of each jacket front, tack a line of small stitches between the pocket markings, extending 2cm (¾in) either side of the openings. Tack parallel lines of equal length, 3mm (⅛in) above and below the centre line. With right sides together, position each pocket flap with the bottom pointing towards the neckline and the stitching line aligned with the upper marked pocket line.

4 With right sides together, pin each pocket piece over the guide lines so that the straight edge of the pocket is 2.5cm (1in) beneath the lower tacked guide line.

5 Turn the garment to the wrong side. Using a short machine stitch and precisely following the markings, stitch around the

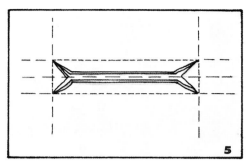

rectangle, starting and finishing halfway across a long side. Slash along the centre tacked line through all thicknesses, stopping 1cm (⅜in) from each end and then cutting diagonally into the corners.

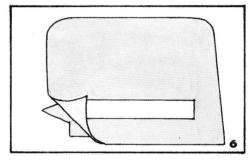

6 Push each patch through to the wrong side, and turn the flap down to cover the opening. Press all seam allowances away from the opening.

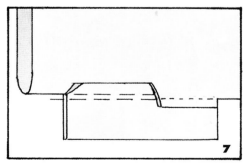

7 Turn the garment to the right side. Flip the bottom edge up to expose the raw edge of the pocket seam. Slip the pocket lining underneath, matching raw edges at the bottom. Stitch close to the garment. Press the seam allowance back away from the pocket opening. Trim the seam allowance. Repeat for the other pocket.

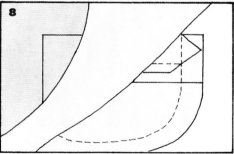

8 Turn the garment to the wrong side. Press down the pocket lining section. Turn the upper pocket section down over the opening; pin to the lining, matching the raw edges. Working from the right side, tack and stitch around the pocket. Trim the raw edges and zigzag to finish. Press flat. Repeat for the other pocket. If desired, make bar tacks at the pocket corners: sew three threads across each corner and then cover the

threads with blanket stitch which just catches the fabric beneath.

BACK AND SHOULDER SEAMS

9 With right sides together, pin, tack and stitch the centre back seam. Press the seam flat, then notch the curves and press the seam open. With right sides together, join the back and front sections at the shoulder seams. Press the seams flat and then press them open.

FRONT FACINGS, COLLAR AND FRONT SIDE SEAMS

10 With right sides together, join the back neck facing at the centre seam. Press the seam open. With right sides together join the front facings to the back neck facing at

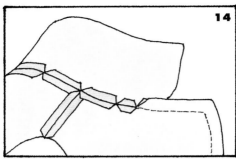

notch the curves and diagonally trim the points. Press all facing seam allowances back onto the garment.

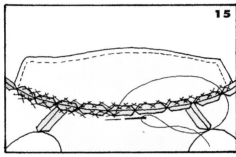

15 On the undercollar neckline, catch both sides of the seam allowance to the garment and interfacing with herringbone stitch.

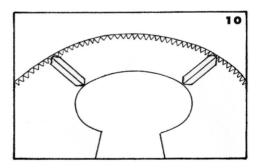

the shoulders. Press the seams open. Zigzag stitch the entire facing unit around the inside edge.

11 Take one collar piece (now called the upper collar) and pin, tack and stitch it to the facing along the neck edge, matching dots and easing to fit. Remove the tacking. Press the seam flat using just the tip of the iron. Notch the curves then press the seam open, again using just the tip of the iron.

12 Iron interfacing to the wrong side of the remaining collar section (now called the under-collar). With right sides together, attach the under-collar to the garment body in the same way as for the upper collar.

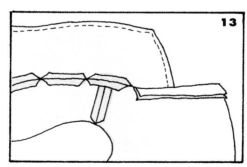

13 With right sides together, join the under-collar to the upper collar, turning the neckline seam allowances down towards the garment. Stitch and press flat.

14 Flip the neckline seam allowances up and join the lapel and front edges together in the usual way. Press flat. Trim the seams,

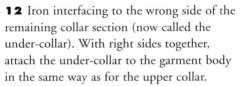

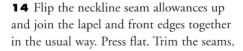

16 Turn the facings to the wrong side, gently easing out points and curves. Press, rolling the facing edge very slightly under. For a professional finish, pick stitch around the fronts, lapels and collar, to hold the facing edge close to the garment and prevent a puffy effect. Pick stitch is a backstitch with a very small stitch visible and a much longer stitch invisible. It is worked on the facing surfaces close to the seam edge, through to the seam allowance beneath. It does not actually connect with the upper face of the garment.

17 Join the remaining side seams together in the usual way, and zigzag the remaining jacket raw edge at the hem.

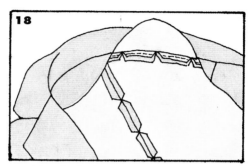

18 Turn back the lapels along the marked lines, and roll the collar back to make a smooth line. Pin and tack along the roll line and directly above the back neck seamline. Lift the back facing up and catch the facing seam allowance to the under-collar seam allowance as they have come to rest during the pinning.

19 On the straight edges, catch the facings to the interfacings for about 5cm (2in). Gently press the lapels and collar, remembering to remove the tacking as you go. Slip a pencil-thin roll of fabric between the two inner surfaces of the roll line, to ensure it has a nice spring.

BOTTOM HEM

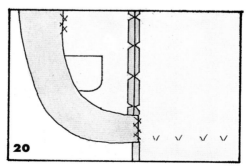

20 Iron a strip of interfacing just inside the hemline on the wrong side of the jacket lower edge; it should be about 3mm (1/8 in)

deeper than the hem itself. Matching seams, turn up the hem along the hemline, and tack. Press lightly to shrink the hem to fit the curve. Herringbone stitch the hem to the garment, and the facing side edges to the hem. Press.

SLEEVES

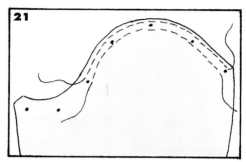

21 Iron a 3cm (1¼in) deep strip of interfacing just inside the hemline on the wrong side of the sleeve lower edge. Zigzag the sleeve lower edge. Make two lines of running stitches between dots on the sleeve head, leaving the ends free. Join the sleeve seam in the usual way, matching notches and dots. Notch the curves and press the seams open. Turn up the hem and herringbone stitch into place. Repeat for the other sleeve.

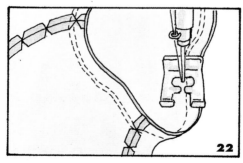

22 With the right sides together and matching the sleeve seam to the jacket back side seam, draw up the threads of the running stitches until the dots on the sleeve head match those on the jacket armhole. Pin, tack and stitch 1cm (⅜in) from the edge. Stitch again just inside the first stitching. Press the stitching only, using

the tip of the iron. Trim the fabric as close to the stitching as possible, and zigzag stitch raw edge to finish. Do not clip curves. Repeat this step for the other sleeve.

23 Catch the facings to the jacket at the centre back and shoulder seams with herringbone stitch.

BUTTONHOLES

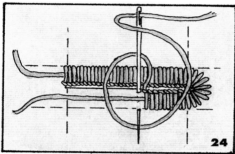

24 The buttonholes should be made on the left front, this is the traditional side for gentlemen. Following your markings, make them either by machine or by hand. For a hand-made buttonhole, first mark it out very accurately, using small stitches through both layers of fabric. Slash the fabric down the centre, only as far as the vertical markers. Overcast the raw edges all around. Using the markings as a guide, buttonhole stitch neatly to cover both raw edges. Fan the stitches out around a curve on the fastening edge, and make a bar tack (see step 8) to finish the inner end. If you run a thread along the outer surface of the buttonhole and work over it, this will create a tailored effect. Tie the loose thread ends together at the back before covering the bar tack.

CONSTRUCTING THE LINING

25 Join the centre back seam along the dotted line. Trim the seam, notch and press flat. Tack along the solid line. (When the tacking is removed in the next step, this will

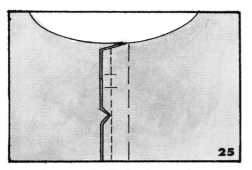

form the centre back pleat.) Press the seam flat and then to one side. Turn to the right side. Make two or three small cross stitches through the entire pleat just below the neckline; repeat at the waistline. Join the remaining lining pieces in exactly the same way as for the jacket.

26 Run a line of machine stitching 6mm (¼in) from the raw edges of the curved fronts and neckline. Clip and notch the curves as necessary. Turn the raw edge back and tack so that the stitching line is just hidden from the right side. Press lightly. Remove the tacking from the centre back pleat.

27 Turn the bottom hem up along the hemline. Matching seams, tack and press the hem very lightly.

ATTACHING THE LINING

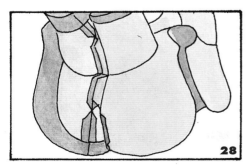

28 Turn both the garment and the lining wrong side out, and position them back to back. Match the sleeve and back side seams of the garment and lining, and use running stitch to catch the seam allowances together

for 7.5cm (3in) down the side and 5cm (2in) down the sleeve. Turn the lining back to cover the wrong side of the garment.

29 Match and pin the lining edge around the neckline and down the fronts. Slipstitch into place. Catch the garment hems together approximately 6mm (¼in) under the lining edge, taking care to catch only the underside of the lining. Turn up and attach the sleeve hem linings in the same way. Press the lining only very lightly.

The waistcoat

CUTTING OUT AND TRANSFERRING MARKINGS

Pin the pattern pieces onto the prepared fabric as directed on the pattern. Cut the pieces out. Transfer all markings from the pattern pieces to the fabric using tailor tacks and running tailor tacks.

POCKETS AND FRONTS

1 Using the front facing pattern, cut out two pieces of iron-on interfacing, trimming away the seam allowances from the opening

edges, shoulder edges and side seams, and iron in place on the wrong side of each waistcoat front.

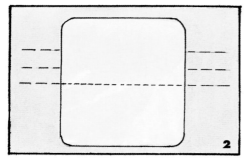

2 Make the pockets as for the jacket, step 3, disregarding the flap instructions. Fold each pocket piece in half horizontally, with right sides together; press. Pin each pocket section over the pocket markings so that the crease aligns with the lower pocket markings.

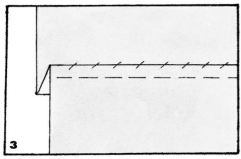

3 Turn the garment to the wrong side and stitch as for the jacket, steps 5 and 6, disregarding the reference to the flap. Fold each lower pocket section up to form a pleat that covers the pocket opening, checking that the fold will actually cover the opening. Tack the edge of the fold, and whipstitch into place on the wrong side.

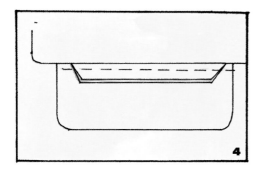

4 Turn the garment to the right side, and flip the lower edge up to expose the pocket and seam allowance. Stitch close to the fold to secure the seam allowance to the pocket. Press. Repeat for the other pocket.

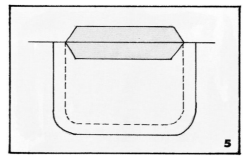

5 Turn the garment to the wrong side. Turn down each pocket portion to match the lower portion. Press the seam allowance open at the top. Pin, tack and stitch as for the jacket, step 8.

BACK AND SHOULDER SEAMS

6 With right sides together, join the centre back seam. Press the seam flat, notch the curves and press the seam open. With right sides together, join the fronts to the back at the shoulders. Press the seams open.

FACINGS

7 Join the centre back neck facing. Join the waistcoat front facings to the back facing at the shoulders. Press the seams open. Zigzag around the inner facing edge if necessary.

8 With right sides together and matching centre backs, shoulders and edges, pin, tack and stitch the facing to the garment. Check that the front edges and angles match, then stitch diagonally over the corners. Notch the curves and trim the seams. Press the facing seam allowances away from the edges, back to the garment.

9 Turn the facing to the wrong side. Ease out the points and curves, and press the neckline and fronts. Lightly catch the front facing to the interfacing for 2.5cm (1in).

Catch the facings to the seam allowances at the shoulders and at centre back. Run a line of machine stitching 6mm (¼in) from the raw edge of the back waistcoat hem.

LINING

10 Join the centre back seam and shoulders of the lining as for the waistcoat, step 6.

11 Run a line of machine stitching 6mm (¼in) from the raw edges around the neckline and front edges and across the back hem edge. Fold back the raw edges, tack and press so that the stitching line is just hidden from the right side. Leave the back hem untacked.

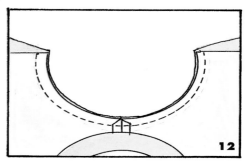

12 With right sides together, pin, tack and stitch the lining to the waistcoat around the armhole edges. Press, notch the curves and trim the seam. Turn the lining to the inside, and press the armhole seams.

SIDE SEAMS, HEMS AND FINISHING

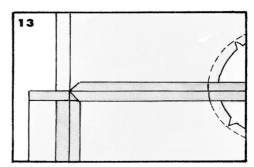

13 At each armhole side seam, spread out the waistcoat and lining. With right sides together, join the armhole seam together so

that lining meets lining and garment meets garment. Press the seam open, and press the facing flap back.

14 Turn the lining back to the garment, matching the side seams. Press. Pin, tack and slipstitch the lining to the garment. Make buttonholes as marked, by machine or by hand, as for the jacket, step 24.

The bow-tie

CUTTING OUT AND TRANSFERRING MARKINGS

Pin the pattern pieces onto the prepared fabric as directed on the pattern. Cut the pieces out. Transfer all markings from the pattern pieces to the fabric using tailor tacks and running tailor tacks.

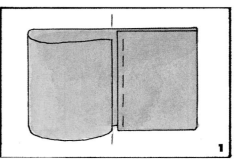

1 With right sides together, fold the bow section in half lengthwise. Sew down the long edge. Press the seam open. Turn right side out and press. Fold the raw edges back to meet at the centre back. Tack the raw edges to the front.

2 Make two lines of running stitches down the centre through all layers. Draw up the threads and secure.

3 With right sides together, fold the remaining strips in half lengthwise. Stitch, press and turn right side out. Tuck in the raw edges at both ends of the long strip, and slipstitch closed.

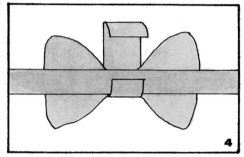

4 Place the long strip horizontally along the back of the bow. Place the short strip centrally around the gathered section. Cut the excess length away, and turning under the raw edge, fasten the band to encircle both the bow and its tie. Cut away any excess, and sew the ends together under the raw edge. Overlapping the ends of the long strip by 1.25cm (½in), sew the two halves of a press-stud to the ends.

Lady's DRESS AND JACKET

Linen is a notorious culprit for creasing, so a linen-look fabric has been used for this easy-fitting style. The sleeveless dress has unpressed box pleats at the front and back and contrast buttons at the front opening. The pure wool edge-to-edge jacket is styled short so as not to interfere with shopping bags. It is lined with the same mustard-coloured pure silk as the yoke of the dress.

FABRIC REQUIREMENTS

FABRIC WIDTH	90cm (36in)	115cm (45in)	136cm (54in)	150cm (60in)
DRESS	50cm (½yd)	50cm (½yd)	30cm (¼yd)	30cm (¼yd)
DRESS LINING	30cm (¼yd)	30cm (¼yd)	30cm (¼yd)	30cm (¼yd)
JACKET	50cm (½yd)	50cm (½yd)	30cm (¼yd)	30cm (¼yd)
JACKET LINING	30cm (¼yd)	30cm (¼yd)	30cm (¼yd)	30cm (¼yd)

TO FINISH

DRESS	Matching sewing thread
JACKET	Matching sewing thread • Iron-on interfacing • 2 buttons

See page 109–110 for pattern templates

The dress

CUTTING OUT AND TRANSFERRING MARKINGS

Pin the pattern pieces onto the prepared fabric as directed on the pattern. Cut the pieces out. Transfer all markings from the pattern pieces to the fabric using tailor tacks and running tailor tacks.

YOKE

1 With right sides together, join the front yoke sections to the back yoke section at the shoulders. Press to sink the stitches, and press the seams open. Repeat this step with the corresponding lining pieces.

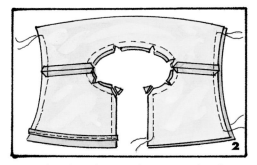

2 With right sides together, pin and tack the lining to the yoke around the armholes and the neck and front edges, stopping short 1cm (⅜in) before the beginning and end of each seam. Using a smaller machine stitch, stitch diagonally across the corners at the neckline opening. Press. Clip and notch the curves and clip the corners. Press the seam allowances open. Turn under a 6mm (¼in) hem along the bottom edges of the yoke lining sections, and tack close to the edge. Clip the curves just short of the very hem edge. Turn the whole yoke right side out, easing out the corners. Press.

FRONT OPENING AND SKIRT PLEATS

3 Zigzag around all raw edges of both skirt front pieces except for the tops. With right sides together, join the centre front seam from the dot to the hem. Press the seam to

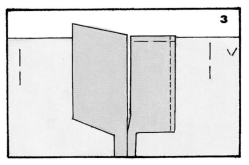

sink the stitches. Press the seam open, and continue to press the opening edge on the right-hand skirt front. Turn under a 6mm (¼in) hem along the raw edge of the facing. Tack the facing to the skirt at the top.

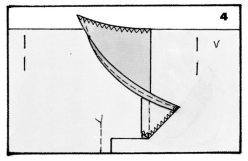

4 Turn under a 6mm (¼in) hem along the long raw edge of the skirt facing section, and zigzag the two short raw edges. With right sides together, stitch the remaining long raw edge of the facing to the facing flap on the left side of the skirt opening. Press. Trim the seam allowance as necessary. Press the seam open and then press the entire seam away from the opening. Fold the facing flap along the seamline, and tack to the garment at the waist top.

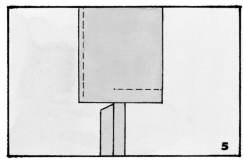

5 Clip the left front seam allowance to the seamline immediately below the opening,

and press. Tack all three layers of facing together at the bottom of the opening. Machine stitch them together as far as the seamline. Press.

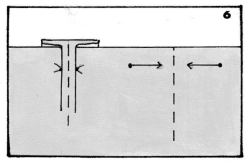

6 Still working from the wrong side, make the pleats in the skirt front and back, making a fold at each dot and taking it to the line, as indicated on the pattern. Tack each pleat in place.

SKIRT SIDE SEAMS AND ARMHOLE FACINGS

7 With right sides together, join the skirt front to the skirt back at the side seams. Press the seams open.

8 Zigzag around each curved edge of the armhole facings and turn under a 6mm (¼in) hem. Machine stitch and press. With right sides together, match the armhole facings to the garment armholes. Stitch and press. Clip the curves. Press the facing allowances away from the armhole edges. Turn the facings to the wrong side of the garment and tack in place at the skirt tops. Catch the facings to the skirt where they cross the side seams.

ATTACHING THE SKIRT TO THE YOKE

9 With the right sides together, match the skirt front to the front yoke, and the skirt back to the back yoke. Tack and machine stitch in place. Remove the tacking and any remaining tailor tacks. Press the seams open, and then press them up towards the yoke. Trim the seam allowances as necessary. On the wrong side, slipstitch the tacked yoke hems to just cover the yoke/skirt seamline. Remove the tacking and press.

FINISHING

10 Turn the hem under at the marked hemline. Tack and herringbone stitch into place, taking care to prevent the stitches from showing on the right side. Press lightly.

11 With the garment right side out, make two buttonholes by hand or machine at the markings on the left front yoke. Press lightly. Sew the buttons to the right yoke front in the corresponding positions.

The jacket

CUTTING OUT AND TRANSFERRING MARKINGS

Pin the pattern pieces onto the prepared fabric as directed on the pattern. Cut the pieces out. Transfer all markings from the pattern pieces to the fabric using tailor tacks and running tailor tacks.

JACKET BODY AND FACINGS

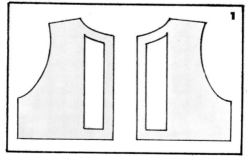

1 Place a 3 x 11cm (1¼ x 4¼in) strip of iron-on interfacing just up to the seamline on the wrong side of each jacket front, and iron in place following the manufacturer's instructions.

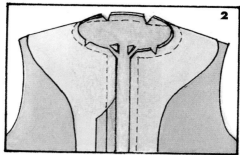

2 With right sides together, join the jacket fronts to the jacket back at the shoulders. Press to sink the stitches and press the seams open. With right sides together join the jacket front facings to the back neck facing at the shoulders, and press the seams as before. Zigzag around the entire curved edge of the facing.

3 With right sides together, and matching the shoulder seams and front and neck edges, pin, tack and stitch the facing to the garment. Stitch diagonally across the corner points and press. Clip diagonally across the corners. Clip and notch the curves as necessary. Press the facing allowances open. Turn the facing back to the wrong side of the garment, easing out the corners, and press into place.

SLEEVES AND SIDE SEAMS

4 On the wrong side of each sleeve, iron on a 6mm (¼in) deep strip of interfacing just behind the hem foldline, stopping the strip short of the seam allowance at each side. Zigzag the bottom raw edges of the sleeves.

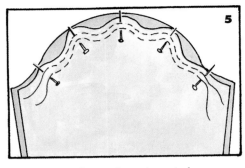

5 Make two lines of running stitches between the dots on the sleeve headings. With right sides together, pin the sleeve heads to the garment armholes, matching the dots. Draw up the gathers until the

sleeve heads fit neatly into the armholes. Adjust the fabric to eliminate folds and pleats. Pin and tack. Machine stitch 1cm (⅜in) from the edge. Stitch again just inside the first stitching. Trim close to the stitching, and zigzag the entire seam edge. Press the stitching only.

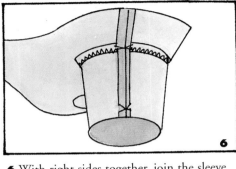

6 With right sides together, join the sleeve and body side seams. Press. Press the seam open, clipping into the allowance at an angle at the hemline marking.

7 Turn the sleeve hems up along the marked hemline and herringbone stitch them in place, taking care to prevent the stitches from showing on the right side. Press the hems.

LOWER HEM AND FACINGS

8 Zigzag across the entire raw edge of the hem. Cut a 35.5 x 2.2cm (14 x ⅞in) strip of iron-on interfacing and iron it in position just behind the marked hemline. Turn up the hem along the marked line and tack, omitting the facings. Herringbone stitch the hem in place. Remove the tacking and press.

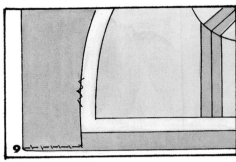

9 Fold the hem edges of the front facings back to their correct positions, making sure that the bottom edges don't show below the garment hemline. Slipstitch the two bottom edges together, and herringbone stitch the facings to the garment where they pass over the hem. Continue to herringbone stitch the facings to the garment for 4cm (1½in) beyond the hem. Press.

10 Catch the shoulder facings to the shoulder seams with a few hand stitches. Press lightly.

LINING

11 Join the front and back lining sections together in exactly the same way as for the jacket. Turn under and tack a 6mm (¼in) hem around the front openings and the neck edge. Tack close to the edge and lightly clip the curves.

12 Insert the sleeve linings into the armholes and join the side seams in exactly the same way as for the jacket. Turn up and tack a hem along the marked hemline on the sleeves, and also at the marked hemline across the bottom.

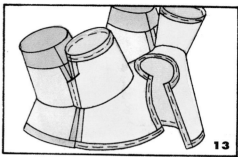

13 Place the garment and the lining back to back, with both wrong side out, matching the underarm and side seams of the jacket and lining. Using running stitch and keeping the seam allowances flat against each other, catch them together for about 2.5cm (1in) down each sleeve.

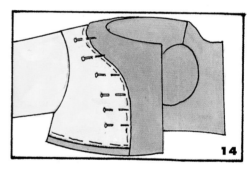

14 Pull the lining over the garment sleeves so that the lining is right side out and covers the wrong side of the jacket. Pin the lining carefully into place, matching the shoulder seams and side seams to the jacket. Pin and tack the items into position. Catch the lining to the garment hem about 3mm (⅛in) under the lining hem edge. Slipstitch the lining to the garment around the front opening and neckline. Smooth the lining very gently with the iron.

Gentleman's
EVENING OUTFIT

Silver encircles the neck and marks the opening of this silver-grey full-sleeved tunic shirt. The wrists sparkle silver and the loose tunic is caught about the waist with a fine black cord. The subtle dark-grey brocade jerkin, figured in arcs and swirls of black, falls from a proud high collar of tightly embossed black brocade, the whole laid over a lining of whispering black. Embossed black velvet, blending into night-time shadows, forms the hat, which is trimmed with a gold-decorated band.

FABRIC WIDTH	90cm (36in)	115cm (45in)	136cm (54in)	150cm (60in)
SHIRT	1m (1yd)	70cm (¾yd)	70cm (¾yd)	70cm (¾yd)
JERKIN	70cm (¾yd)	70cm (¾yd)	70cm (¾yd)	50cm (½yd)
JERKIN LINING	50cm (½yd)	50cm (½yd)	50cm (½yd)	50cm(½yd)
HAT	30cm (¼yd)	30cm (¼yd)	30cm (¼yd)	30cm (¼yd)
HAT LINING	30cm (¼yd)	30cm (¼yd)	30cm (¼yd)	30cm (¼yd)
ORNAMENTAL BAND FOR HAT	30cm (¼yd)	30cm (¼yd)	30cm (¼yd)	30cm (¼yd)

TO FINISH

SHIRT	Iron-on interfacing • Contrast fabric for collar, facing and cuffs • 2 press studs • 1.4m (1½yd) ornamental cord • Matching sewing thread
JERKIN	Matching sewing thread
HAT	Matching sewing thread

See page 111–115 for pattern templates

The evening tunic shirt

CUTTING OUT AND TRANSFERRING MARKINGS

Pin the pattern pieces onto the prepared fabric as directed on the pattern. Cut the pieces out. Transfer all markings from the pattern pieces to the fabric using tailor tacks and running tailor tacks.

FRONTS AND PLACKET

1 Cut two 1 x 14cm (⅜ x 5½in) strips of iron-on interfacing. Press one strip onto the wrong side of the left front, butting it up to the foldline and trimming away 6mm (¼in) from the neckline edge. Turn under and

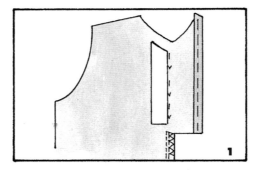

tack a 6mm (¼in) hem along the front opening edge.

2 Iron the second strip of interfacing onto the wrong side of the facing section, butting it up to the stitching line on the long edge. Turn under and tack a 6mm (¼in) hem

along the opposite long edge and across the bottom.

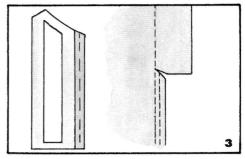

3 With right sides together, pin, tack and stitch the two front sections together at the off-centre front seam, matching dots and hemline markings. Stitch again just inside the first stitching. Trim close to the stitching and zigzag the edge. Clip diagonally into the corner and press the seam to one side.

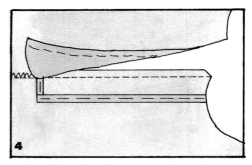

4 Matching the edges, pin and tack the right side of the facing section to the wrong side of the garment at the remaining opening edge. Stitch. Press the seam allowances away from the garment. Fold the facing over to the front of the garment and hem in place.

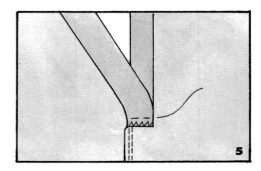

5 Turn the facing along the foldline on the opposite front and hem it to the wrong side of the garment. Zigzag the remaining raw edge at the base of the placket, and catch the placket together at the base. Press.

6 With right sides together, join the fronts to the backs at the shoulders, with two lines of stitching followed by zigzag stitching as in step 3. Press the seams flat and then press them towards the shirt back.

COLLAR

7 Iron a 1.5cm (⅝in) wide strip of interfacing to the wrong side of the collar, butting it up against the central foldline, and leaving it 6mm (¼in) short at either end. Turn under 6mm (¼in) along the remaining long collar edge, and tack.

8 With right sides together, pin, tack and stitch the interfaced side of the collar to the garment neckline. Clip the allowances, press the seam open, and then press them away from the garment.

9 Fold the collar along the foldline with right sides together. Stitch the ends. Press. Clip the corners diagonally, and turn the collar right side out. Carefully ease out the corners, press then slipstitch the collar to the wrong side of the garment at the neckline seam. Press.

SLEEVES

10 Make two parallel lines of running stitches between the dots at the sleeve head, and do the same along the bottom edge of the sleeve.

11 Prepare the cuff in the same way as for the collar in step 7. With right sides together, pin the interfaced portion of the cuff to the lower edge of the sleeve. Draw up the threads of the running stitches so that the sleeve fits across the cuff. Tack and stitch. Remove the tacking and running

stitches. Press the seam and cuff away from the garment. Repeat the procedure for the other sleeve and cuff.

12 With right sides together, pin the sleeve into the armhole at the dots. Pull up the threads of the running stitches to fit the armhole, distributing the gathers evenly. Tack and stitch 1cm (⅜in) from the edge,

making two lines of stitching followed by zigzag stitching as in step 3. Press the stitching only, and then press the seam allowance towards the sleeve. Repeat for the other sleeve.

13 With right sides together and matching the underarm seams, hemline markings and cuff seams, stitch the entire side and

pattern pieces to the fabric using tailor tacks and running tailor tacks.

FACINGS AND SHOULDER SEAMS

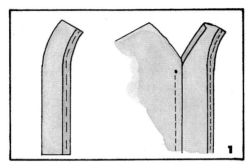

1 Turn under a 6mm (¼in) hem along the inner curved edge of the front facings; stitch and press. With right sides together, pin, tack and stitch the front facings to the front garment sections, from the dot to the hem. Press the seams away from the garment, then press back the remaining facing allowance, continuing the seamline.

2 With right sides together, join the front sections to the back at the shoulders. Press the seams flat and then open.

COLLAR

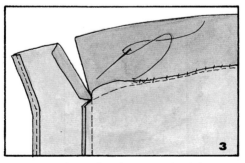

3 Turn under and tack a 6mm (¼in) hem along the neckline edge of one collar section. With right sides together, join the two collar sections, reinforcing the collar corners with smaller stitching. Press. Clip the curves and clip diagonally across the corners. Press the seams open, and then turn the collar right side out and press.

underarm seam on each side, again using two rows of stitching followed by zigzag stitching as in step 3.

14 Turn each cuff at the foldline and slipstitch in place on the wrong side of the garment along the seamline. Remove any markings and tacking, then press.

HEM AND FINISHING

15 Turn under the hem at the foldline. Tack in place and then hem to the garment. Remove any tacking, and press.

16 Sew press studs to the neck opening at the marked positions. Knot the length of cord at either end and wrap it twice around the gentleman's waist to form a belt. Tie it so that the ends hang below the off-centre shirt opening.

The jerkin

CUTTING OUT AND TRANSFERRING MARKINGS

Pin the pattern pieces onto the prepared fabric as directed on the pattern. Cut the pieces out. Transfer all markings from the

4 With right sides together, pin, tack and stitch the untacked edge of the collar to the garment at the neckline. Press, and clip the curves. Press the seam open, and then press it back up towards the collar, away from the garment. Slipstitch the tacked collar edge fractionally above the neckline stitching, on the wrong side of the garment.

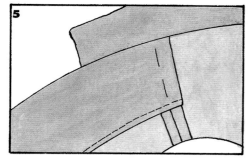

5 Press the front facings back to the wrong side of the garment and slipstitch the folded neckline edge to the collar edge. Tack across the shoulder area.

LINING

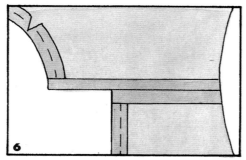

6 Make a line of machine stitching around the neck edge of the lining back section, 6mm (¼in) in from the edge. Clip the curves and turn under a hem along this stitching line. Tack in place. Turn under a 6mm (¼in) hem along the front opening edges of both front sections; tack. With right sides together, join the fronts to the back at the shoulders. Press the seams flat and then open, continuing to press back the seam allowance of the back lining.

ATTACHING THE LINING

7 With right sides together, and matching shoulder seams and edges, pin and tack the lining to the garment around the armhole edges. Stitch 6mm (¼in) from the edge. Press, clip the curves and press the seams open. Turn the garment right side out, so that both wrong sides face each other. Press the armhole edges.

8 With right sides together, join the side seam of the lining front and back, and the garment front and back, into one continuous seam, being careful to match the underarm seam. Press the seam flat and then press it open. Do the same for the remaining side seam. Turn the garment the correct way round again, and press the side seam onto itself at the armhole edge. Slipstitch the tacked lining edge to the collar edge at the back neckline, and across the front facings at the shoulders.

HEMS AND FINISHING

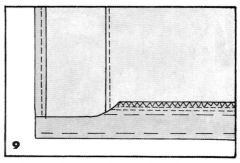

9 Zigzag the entire lower edge of garment and lining. Turn each hem under at the hemline markings, rolling the lining so the markings are fractionally above the hemline, to prevent the lining from peeping below the finished garment. Tack close to each hem edge. On the lining, turn the raw edge under again and, easing the fabric to fit neatly, tack and stitch the hem in place.

10 On the garment hem, tack close to the zigzagged edge, easing and shrinking the fabric into place. Cut away 6mm (¼in) from

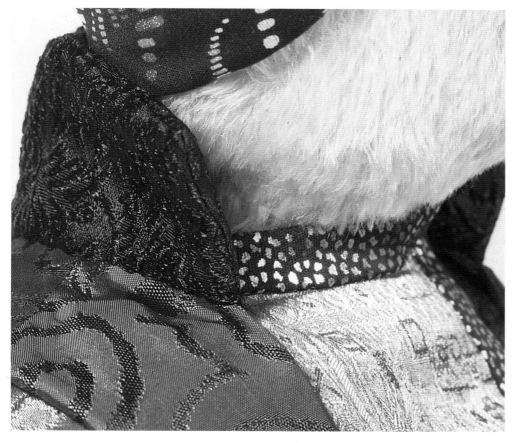

the hem across the facings. Herringbone stitch the entire hem in place. Remove all tacking and press both hems.

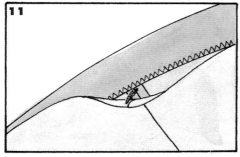

11 Pin and tack the remainder of the lining to the front facings, and slipstitch in place.

At the side seams, catch the lining to the hem of the garment with a few threads, so that they form a short bar. Blanket stitch the bar and then secure the thread. Remove all markings and tacking; press.

The evening hat

CUTTING OUT

Pin the pattern pieces onto the prepared fabric as directed on the pattern. Cut the pieces out.

HEAD SECTION AND LINING

1 Fold the head section of the hat so that the right sides are together, and stitch the short side seam. Press the seam flat and then press it open. Join the resulting tube across one end, keeping the side seam strictly to the side. Press the seam flat and then press it open. Leave the corners unclipped. Turn the hat right side out.

2 Make the lining in exactly the same way, then slip it inside the hat, so that the wrong sides of the hat and lining are together. Match the side seams and tack the lining to the hat around the entire lower edge.

ORNAMENTAL BAND

3 Fold the fabric over so that the right sides are together, and stitch the short side seam. Press the seam flat and then press it open. Turn the hat inside out and, with the right side of the band facing the lining, pin, tack and stitch the edge of the entire tube around the bottom edge of the hat. Press the seam open, and then press it towards the band.

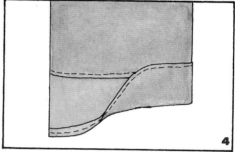

4 Turn under and tack a 6mm (¼in) hem along the remaining lower edge of the band. Fold the band over to the right side of the hat, and tack and stitch it to the hat stitching line. Remove tacking and press.

5 Catch the lining to the hat at the centre of the crown with a few invisible stitches. To wear, push the crown down inside the tube. Turn the band up a second time on the right side of the hat, to make a neat ornamental band.

Lady's EVENING OUTFIT

The dress is crêpe-backed satin of snowy whiteness, falling in unpressed pleats from a bodice with a high neck decked in silver. Graceful sleeves with silver armlets are caught into silvered cuffs, and flashing silver encircles the hem. Like evening shadow, indigo organdie overlays a white satin overbodice. It twinkles here and there with sequin lights which catch the colours of the random pale pink flower buds and green leaves scattered over the organdie.

FABRIC REQUIREMENTS

FABRIC WIDTH	90cm (36in)	115cm (45in)	136cm (54in)	150cm (60in)
DRESS	1m (1yd)	70cm (¾yd)	70cm (¾yd)	50cm (½yd)
BODICE LINING	30cm (⅓yd)	30cm (⅓yd)	30cm (⅓yd)	30cm (⅓yd)
OVERBODICE	30cm (⅓yd)	30cm (⅓yd)	30cm (⅓yd)	30cm (⅓yd)
OVERBODICE LINING	30cm (⅓yd)	30cm (⅓yd)	30cm (⅓yd)	30cm (⅓yd)

TO FINISH

DRESS	Iron-on interfacing • 4 press studs • 2.5m (2³/₄yd) Ornamental braid • Matching sewing thread
OVERBODICE	4 hook and loop eyes • Sequins (optional) • Matching sewing thread

See page 116–117 for pattern templates

The dress

CUTTING OUT AND TRANSFERRING MARKINGS

Pin the pattern pieces onto the prepared fabric as directed on the pattern. Cut the pieces out. Transfer all markings from the pattern pieces to the fabric using tailor tacks and running tailor tacks. Cut the skirt pattern with right sides out.

BODICE AND BODICE LINING

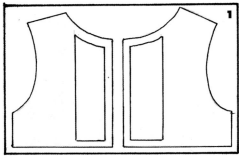

1 Cut two 4cm (1½in) wide strips of iron-on interfacing to match the bodice opening edges. Trim away 6mm (¼in) from the neckline and waistline edges and press to the wrong side of

each front, so that the edge butts up to the sewing line.

2 With right sides together, join the bodice fronts and back together at the shoulders. Press the seams flat and then open. Repeat this step exactly for the lining.

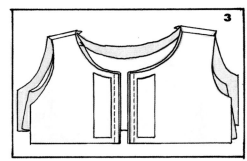

3 With right sides together, match the garment front opening edges to those of the lining. Pin, tack and stitch. Press the seams flat and then open. Turn the sections right side out. Match and tack the bodice to the lining around all the remaining edges.

COLLAR

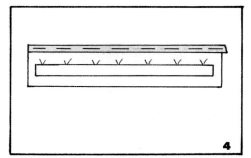

4 Cut a 24 x 1cm (9⅜ x ⅜in) strip of iron-on interfacing. Iron it to the wrong side of the collar section so that it butts up to the foldline, leaving the other long half free. Turn under 6mm (¼in) on the unfaced collar edge, and tack.

5 Tack braid to the interfaced portion of the collar.

ATTACHING THE COLLAR

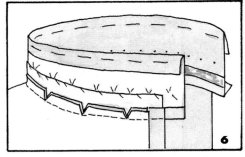

6 With the interfaced collar portion closest to the neckline edge, and with right sides together, pin, tack and stitch the collar to the neckline. Remove the tacking, notch and press the seams open, and then press the entire seamline away from the garment.

7 With right sides together, fold the collar over onto itself at the foldline, and stitch each end together. Press and trim the seams, clipping diagonally at the corners. Turn the collar right side out, ease out the corners and press. Bring the folded edge down to the wrong side of the garment and slipstitch the edge to the neckline seam. Press.

8 Adjusting any irregularities in the placement, hem the tacked braid to the neckline, taking care to avoid any stitching showing on the reverse. Remove the tacking and press.

SLEEVES

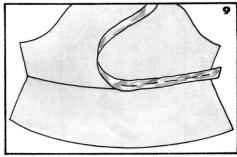

9 With right sides together and easing in any fullness, pin, tack and stitch the shorter edge of the lower sleeve to the bottom of the

ATTACHING SLEEVES

11 Make two parallel lines of running stitches between the dots around the curve of the sleeve head. With right sides together, match and pin the sleeve to the armhole at the dots and centre. Draw up the threads of the running stitches. Pin and tack, manipulating the fabric so as to eliminate any folds. Stitch. Stitch again just inside the first stitching. Trim the seam allowance close to the stitching and zigzag the edge. Press the seam flat, and then press the entire seam towards the sleeve using the tip of the iron. Repeat for the second sleeve.

SLEEVE AND SIDE SEAMS

12 With right sides together, join each sleeve and side seam, matching cuff, braid and underarm seams. Stitch the seam with two rows followed by zigzagging as for step 11. Press the stitching only, and then press the entire seam towards one side using the tip of the iron.

13 With the garment still wrong side out, turn each cuff to the wrong side, notching the seam at the foldline, and slipstitch the tacked edge to the seamline. Turn the garment right side out. Adjusting as you go, hem the braid to each cuff. Remove the tacking and press.

SKIRT

14 With right sides together, stitch the two skirt sections together at the centre back and centre front, from the lower dot to the hem. Stitch two rows followed by zigzagging as for step 11. Press the seam flat, and then press the entire seam towards one side. Clip the seam allowance at the opening junction. Press under 6mm (¼in) on the raw edges of the front opening. Tuck the raw edges under again to form a 3mm (⅛in) hem. Tack and hem into position. Remove tacking; press.

upper sleeve. Stitch again just inside the first stitching. Trim the seam allowance close to the stitching, and zigzag the edge. Press the entire seam towards the top of the sleeve. On the right side of the sleeve, tack and hem braid to the upper side of the seamline. Repeat this step for the second sleeve.

MAKING AND ATTACHING CUFFS

10 Treat both cuffs in exactly the same way as for the collar, steps 4 and 5. Make two parallel lines of running stitches along the bottom edge of each sleeve. With right sides together, pin the remaining raw cuff edges to the sleeve bottoms, drawing up the threads of the running stitches to fit. Spread out the gathers evenly, tack and stitch.

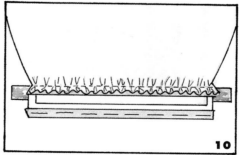

Stitch again just inside the first stitching. Trim the seam allowances close to the stitching. There is no need to zigzag the edges, as they will eventually be encased. Press the entire seam towards the cuff on each sleeve.

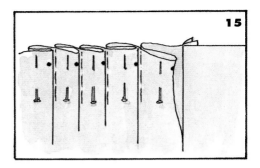

15 Turn the skirt right side out. Beginning at the centre front opening, make each pleat by placing the marking dot to the placement line; pin through all thicknesses. Work to the centre back seam, using the seam as a placement line.

16 In order to keep all the pleats facing in one direction, turn the skirt wrong side out and continue to pleat around the second half of the skirt.

ATTACHING THE SKIRT

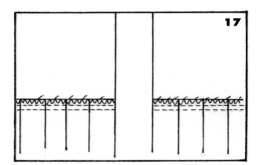

17 With right sides together, pin the pleated skirt to the bodice, adjusting any pleats as necessary to match the two sections together. Tack and stitch a double row followed by zigzagging, as for step 11. Remove all tacking showing on the right side of the garment, and all pleat-marking threads. Press the stitching, and press the entire seam towards the bodice. Hem the seam back to the bodice for about 2.5cm (1in) on either side of the front opening.

HEM AND FASTENINGS

18 Starting at the centre back seam, stitch braid to the right side of the skirt, just above the hemline markings. Press. Fold the hem to the wrong side along the markings. Fold under the raw edge and tack and hem into place. Remove tacking and press.

19 Ensuring that the closure is ladies' style (right front over left), sew small press studs to the front opening edges at the marked positions.

The overbodice

CUTTING OUT AND TRANSFERRING MARKINGS

Use the dress bodice pattern for the overbodice and its lining, but first pin back 6mm (¼in) to the pattern down the front opening edge, and proceed to pin the pattern pieces onto the prepared fabric as

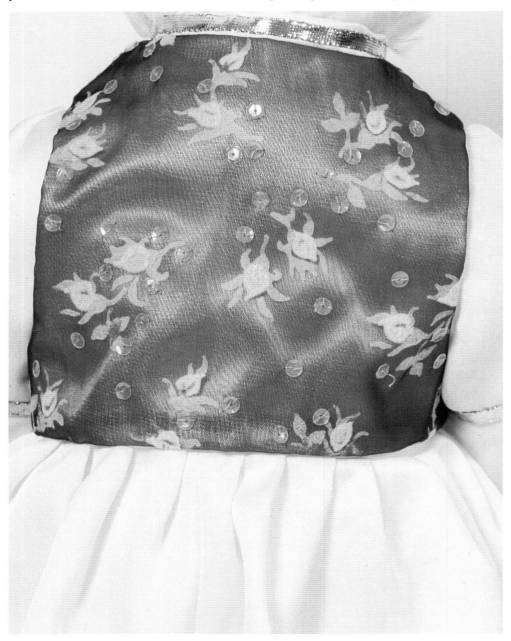

directed on the pattern. Cut the pieces out. Transfer all markings from the pattern pieces to the fabric using tailor tacks and running tailor tacks. Mark in an extra dot to the lower edge of the front opening 3cm (1¼in) beneath the lowest dot.

If you are colouring your satin with organdie, cut out the organdie sections and tack them to the satin around each edge. Treat the two tacked layers as one.

1 With right sides together, join the bodice fronts to the back at the shoulders, and press. Trim the allowances and press the seams open. Do exactly the same for the overbodice lining.

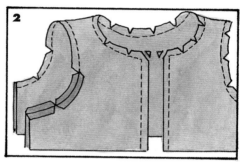

2 With right sides together, pin and stitch the bodice and its lining together around the entire neckline edge. Stitch. Stitch across the corners to reinforce them. Pin and tack the armhole edges together, and stitch 1cm (⅜in) in from the edge. Remove the tacking. Press the seams, trim, clip and notch, and then press the seams open.

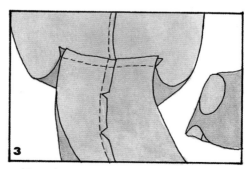

3 Turn the entire garment right side out, easing the fabric carefully through the

shoulder openings. Ease out the points and seam edges, and press. With right sides together, match the side seams, lining to lining and body to body. Stitch, then press the seams open. Fold the garment seams back into position, and press.

4 Turn under and tack a 6mm (¼in) hem along the entire bottom edge of the bodice, keeping the body and lining separate. Apply sequins as required at this point, if you are using them. Slipstitch the two tacked hem

edges together. Remove the tacking and then press.

5 Attach four hooks and loop eyes to the front opening edges, with hooks on the right, loops on the left. Position them at the marked points so that the overbodice meets flush, edge to edge. Press.

Adapting the Patterns

Now that you have the patterns for a basic wardrobe for your bears, you will be able to achieve a variety of different looks simply through your choice of fabrics and how you coordinate and trim the garments.

In addition, by adapting basic patterns, you can create completely different garments. For example, shortening the sleeves of the pyjama top pattern and making it up in a brightly patterned fabric turns it into a *beach shirt*. Similarly, shortening the pattern for the dressing gown and its sleeves, or even omitting the sleeves entirely, will give you a *beach robe*.

Apply a different design to the bib pocket of the dungarees. Shorten the legs dramatically and create a pair of *rompers*. The pyjama bottoms could be transformed into *shorts* by shortening the legs, omitting the fly fastening and inserting a continuous piece of elastic into the waistline heading; or they could be turned into *daytime trousers* simply by pleating the fabric into the waistband. (On any of these you may pleat instead of gather, or gather instead of pleat – the choice is yours.)

Make a new *dress and jacket* from the shopping ensemble by inserting sleeves from the boudoir gown. Omit the jacket sleeves for a loose-fitting *bolero*, lengthening the bolero if you like. Lengthen the bodice of the coat, omitting the coat skirt pattern and straightening the lower edge, to create a sharp little front-fastening *jacket*. Shorten its sleeves to turn it into a *summer jacket* if you wish.

Once you have made a few successful garments from this book, new ideas will spring to mind. Try a few of these adaptations, and even more possibilities will present themselves. This is all part of the creative process.

Always work out which finishing method you are going to use in any altered area, *before* you begin. You may choose any method of armhole finishing given in this book, so long as it is suitable to the fabric and the style.

Should you wish to have a curve at the lower waistcoat edge, rather than hacking into the existing pattern, draw and cut a new pattern with the desired curve. Cut the fronts and back out of old sheeting first, to check that your new line is pleasing to the eye, and if all is well, proceed with the garment. Remember to make new facing and lining patterns as well, to match the new curve exactly.

THE QUESTION OF FIT

Now we come to the vexed question of fit, a subject that has agonized generations of people and, in spite of our computerized world, continues to do so. Just as no two people are exactly alike, so it is with bears. Differences in height, plumpness or otherwise are fairly easily catered for. The additional problem with bears is their construction. Human beings, whatever their shape, size and proportions, are built on a skeleton that is constructed to a universal design. Not so with bears. Their construction can range from methods that allow only severely limited limb movement to others that enable it to be wildly flexible. There is also the fact that the actual position at which each limb is attached to the torso can vary enormously.

However, these factors can be overcome, so long as you consider them when choosing a style, and do not try to force an unsuitable garment onto a bear. For example, it would be a waste of time to make a skirt with a deep waistband for a bear whose legs begin directly beneath the underarm joint. Instead, you should choose a different style of garment to accommodate this feature.

Having said that, many bears are in fact extremely similar in size, proportions and construction, and the chances are that you have bears in your home who are similar to those featured and who could happily wear virtually all of these clothes. For these, any adjustments to fit would be very minor, as explained below. And for bears whose measurements are very different, you can make your own patterns, by following the instructions on pages 84–5.

MAKING A SHELL

Initially, it is worth making up a mock garment, or shell, in sheeting so that you can see where the fit will vary from the pattern. Facings, collars and cuffs can be omitted as these will be determined by any alterations you make.

1 Mark the sheeting with ballpoint pen and cut away the hem allowances, so that you can see where the finished hem will fall on your bear. Tack the pieces together using the same seam allowances as for the actual garment. Now try the shell on the bear and make any necessary adjustments to it.

2 Hem lengths are simple enough to alter: just make a note of the amount by which you will need to shorten or lengthen the garment.

3 If the neckline needs to be deeper, indicate the new sewing line with ballpoint pen and then recut the neckline, allowing a 6mm (¼in) seam allowance. If the neckline needs to be higher, measure and make a note of how much.

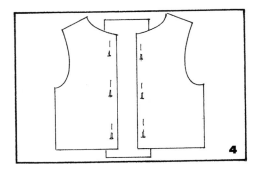

4 To make the back broader or narrower, make the adjustment to the centre back foldline of the garment. If it needs to be broader, slash the back down this foldline and insert a strip of fabric under the slash; pin the slashed edges to the strip to make it the correct width.

5 Making the back broader or narrower may alter the neckline at the shoulders and also how it fits the front shoulder edges. If so, adjust the front and back shoulder edges to match, redrawing the armhole edge if necessary, and reshaping the neckline at the front or back.

6 If you raise or lower the side seams at the armhole, you must make a compensatory adjustment to the sleeve so that you preserve a pleasing fit.

7 Remove the shell garment, undo all the tacking and recut the pattern pieces incorporating all the adjustments. If you have decided to lengthen or shorten any hemlines, mark the new positions and allow the same turn-up depth as on the original pattern. If you have adjusted the width across the back, remember to cut the shell accurately along the centre back.

8 When you have remade the main pattern sections, you will then need to make new pattern sections for facings, collar, cuffs, etc, to fit the adjustments where appropriate. Don't forget to adjust any lining patterns as necessary.

MAKING YOUR OWN PATTERNS

For bears whose measurements are very different from those used for the patterns in this book, you will need to make completely new patterns. If the bear is already sporting a nicely fitting garment which needs replacing, you may unpick the garment and use the pieces as templates for a new pattern. Failing this, you will need to start from scratch – which isn't as difficult as it sounds. You simply make a shell from sheeting, and then make a paper pattern from that.

All clothes can be thought of as bags. They should fit close enough to the body to avoid being cumbersome, yet not so close as to cause serious restriction. Within these precepts fall all the questions of style and purpose that need to be considered.

The following 'draped, cut and pinned' method is not complicated yet will result in nicely fitting garments. It can be used for any garment, but it is usually a good idea to start with something simple, such as a collarless boxy jacket.

To improve your understanding of how a garment is constructed, examine how your own clothes have been put together. Observe how they hang, where the pleats, tucks or gathers occur and why; they may be purely decorative or they may serve to add fullness where the body widens. The more you study these elements, the more experience and confidence you will gain, so that you will soon be able to tackle more complex projects. The cardinal rule for every aspect of sewing and pattern making is to go steady and never rush.

For this procedure, you will need some old sheeting for the shell and some brown paper or non-fusible, medium-weight white interfacing for the pattern.

MAKING A NEW SHELL FOR A PATTERN

1 Cut two rectangles of sheeting which, when curved around the bear, overlap the head, the bottom and beyond the side seams. The straight of grain should run from top to bottom.

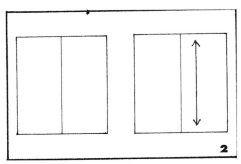

2 Mark the centre line down both pieces along the straight of grain. Mark another line parallel to this on one piece of sheeting; this will be the straight-of-grain marking. Cut along the centre line – you now have the two front pieces.

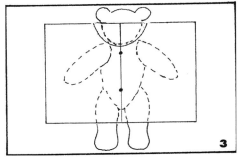

3 Begging the bear's forgiveness, pin the centre back line of the other rectangle to the centre back of the bear. Mark the neckline on the sheeting in ballpoint pen. Cut away the surplus fabric along the neckline. This cut edge will eventually be your seamline. Make a note on the fabric that it is a stitching line, so that you will later remember to add a seam allowance. Do the same to the two front sections, which meet edge to edge down the front of the bear.

4 Pin the front and back fabric sections together at the shoulder seams. Curve the back and front sections around the bear to meet at the side seams.

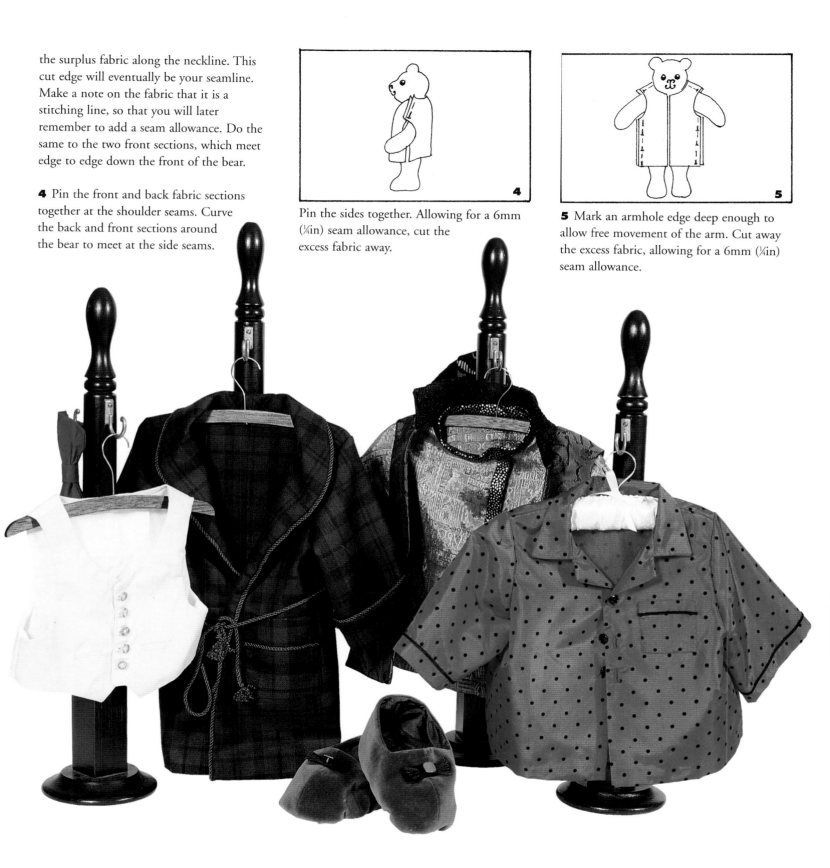

Pin the sides together. Allowing for a 6mm (¼in) seam allowance, cut the excess fabric away.

5 Mark an armhole edge deep enough to allow free movement of the arm. Cut away the excess fabric, allowing for a 6mm (¼in) seam allowance.

6 You now have a basic back and two fronts. Adjust the shell to the bear's neck and torso, raising or lowering the shoulder seams, adjusting the side seams as necessary and checking the ease of fit around the body. When you are satisfied with the fit, mark your final seamlines and hemlines with ballpoint pen. Cut away the hem turn-up so that you have an immediately visible finished edge.

7 To make the sleeve, cut a rectangle of sheeting and fold in half lengthwise along the straight of grain. Beginning approximately two-thirds of the way down, pin the sides of the sleeve together and slip the sleeve over the arm.

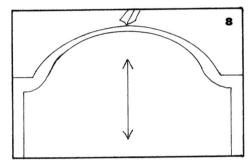

8 Take the centre sleeve line to the top of the shoulder seam, and pin the underarm seam to the underarm side seam of the garment. Remember that the top of the arm and shoulder will require some fullness to accommodate the thicker upper arm and to allow for freedom of movement. Using ballpoint pen, mark on the sleeve heading a curve that follows the armhole edge and comes to its apex at the top of the shoulder. This sleeve edge will be bigger than the armhole edge, and you will eventually shrink the fullness into the armhole during construction.

9 Remove the garment and unpin the side seams. Placing the centre of the sleeve top to the shoulder seam, pin the sleeve into position in the armhole at intervals, to get an idea of the ultimate fit. Repin the side

seams and the underarm sleeve seam, making any adjustments to widen or taper the sleeve. If the sleeve requires more or less fabric at the top, use the slash technique as for step 4 of Making a Shell, page 84, Once you are satisfied with the fit, mark the sleeve hemline and cut away the surplus fabric. Mark all the sewing lines as pinned, with ballpoint pen.

MAKING THE PATTERN PIECES FROM THE SHELL

10 Undo all the pins and any tacking you have used in making the shell. Iron the pieces smooth. Since you will be using only one-half of the back, cut accurately along the centre back line.

11 Cut along any marked stitching lines to eliminate the seam allowances. Secure your fabric pieces to the brown paper or

interfacing with a couple of pins per piece. Mark around each piece, using a ruler on the straight edges. Remember to allow an extra 6mm–1.25cm (¼–½in) at the front opening edge for an overlap for fastenings.

12 Now mark around each pattern piece again, 6mm (¼in) away from the marked stitching lines. Mark the hemlines. Decide what depth of hem you require, and mark the cutting line accordingly. Cut the front and back neck facings from the completed pattern pieces, as it is important for them to be an exact match.

13 Mark the straight-of-grain lines on your pattern pieces. Unless you are making bound buttonholes, there is no need to mark the positions of buttonholes at this stage; this can be done when the garment is complete and the buttons selected.

Templates

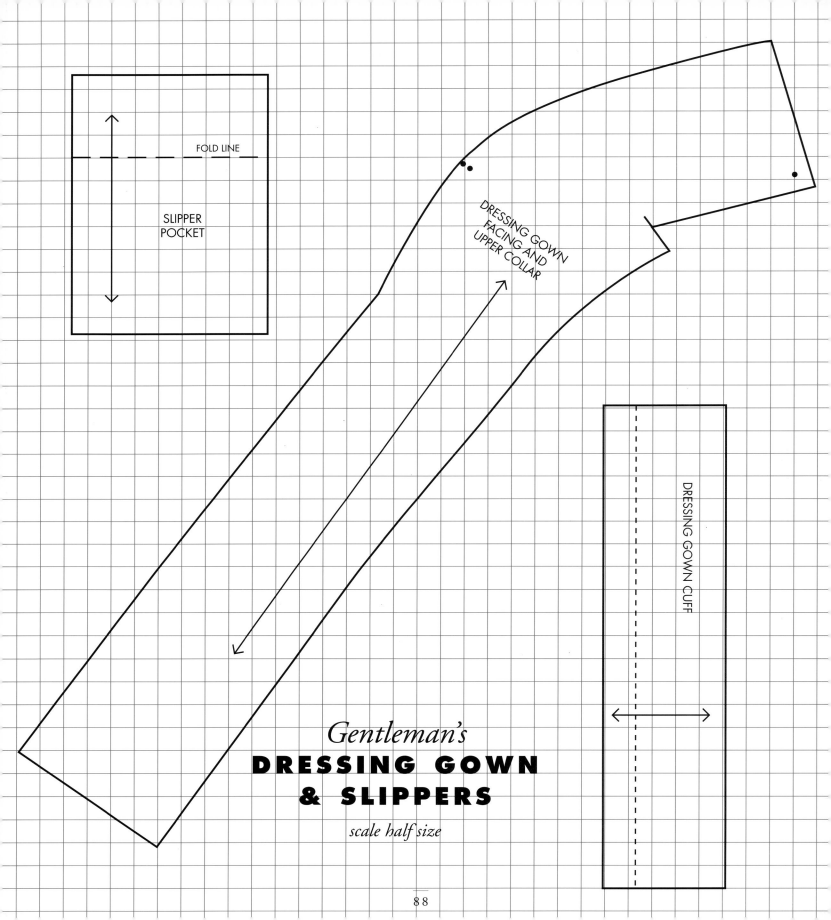

FOLD LINE

SLIPPER
POCKET

DRESSING GOWN
FACING AND
UPPER COLLAR

DRESSING GOWN CUFF

Gentleman's
DRESSING GOWN
& SLIPPERS

scale half size

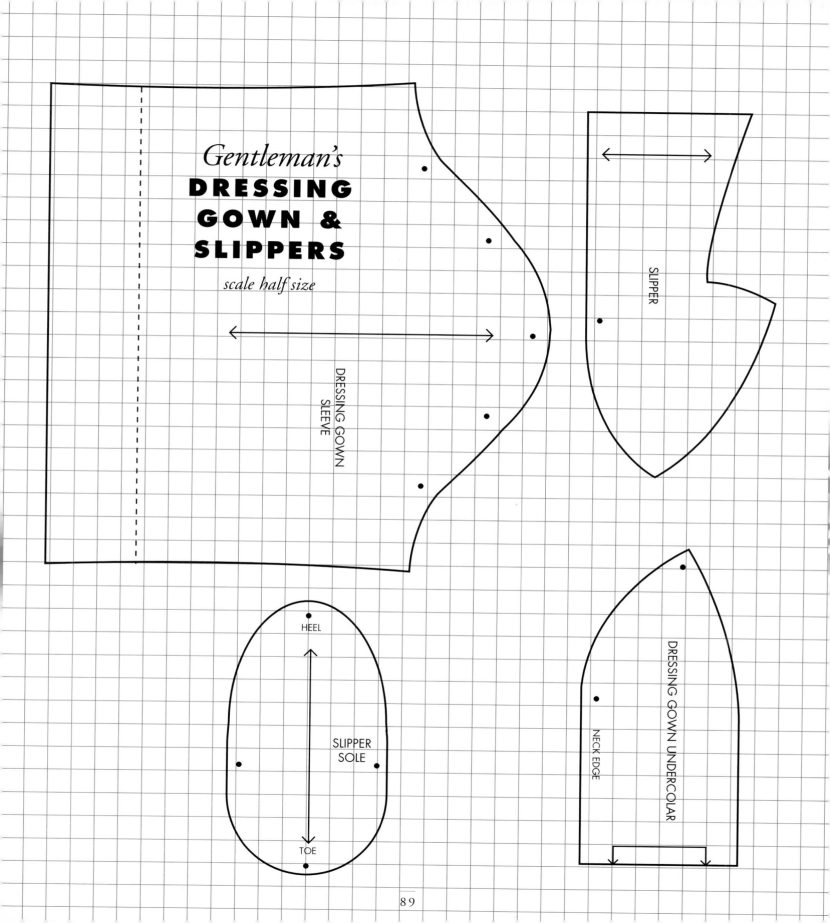

Gentleman's
DRESSING GOWN & SLIPPERS

scale half size

DRESSING GOWN
SLEEVE

SLIPPER

HEEL

SLIPPER
SOLE

TOE

DRESSING GOWN UNDERCOLAR

NECK EDGE

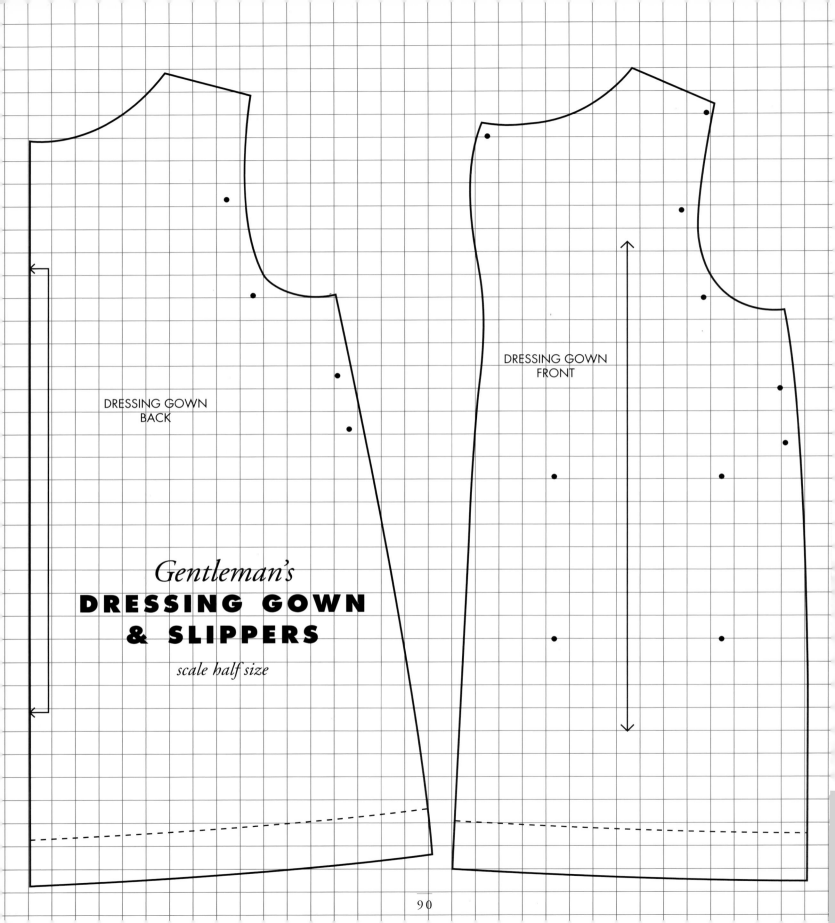

DRESSING GOWN
BACK

DRESSING GOWN
FRONT

Gentleman's
DRESSING GOWN
& SLIPPERS

scale half size

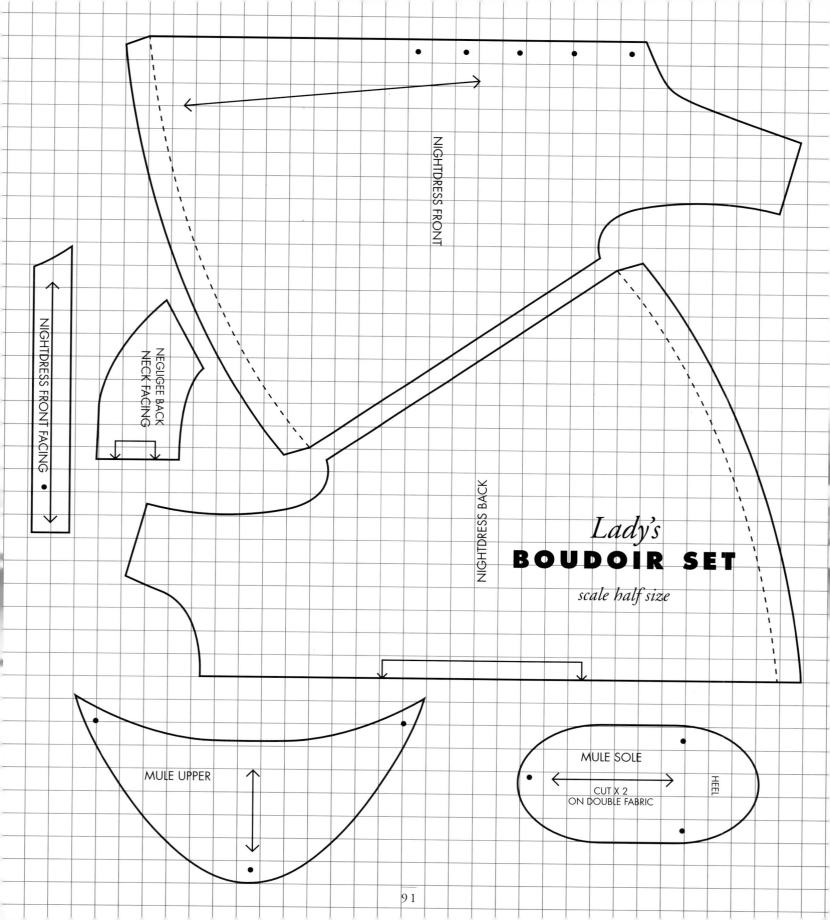

NIGHTDRESS FRONT

NIGHTDRESS FRONT FACING

NEGLIGEE BACK
NECK FACING

NIGHTDRESS BACK

Lady's
BOUDOIR SET

scale half size

MULE UPPER

MULE SOLE

CUT X 2
ON DOUBLE FABRIC

HEEL

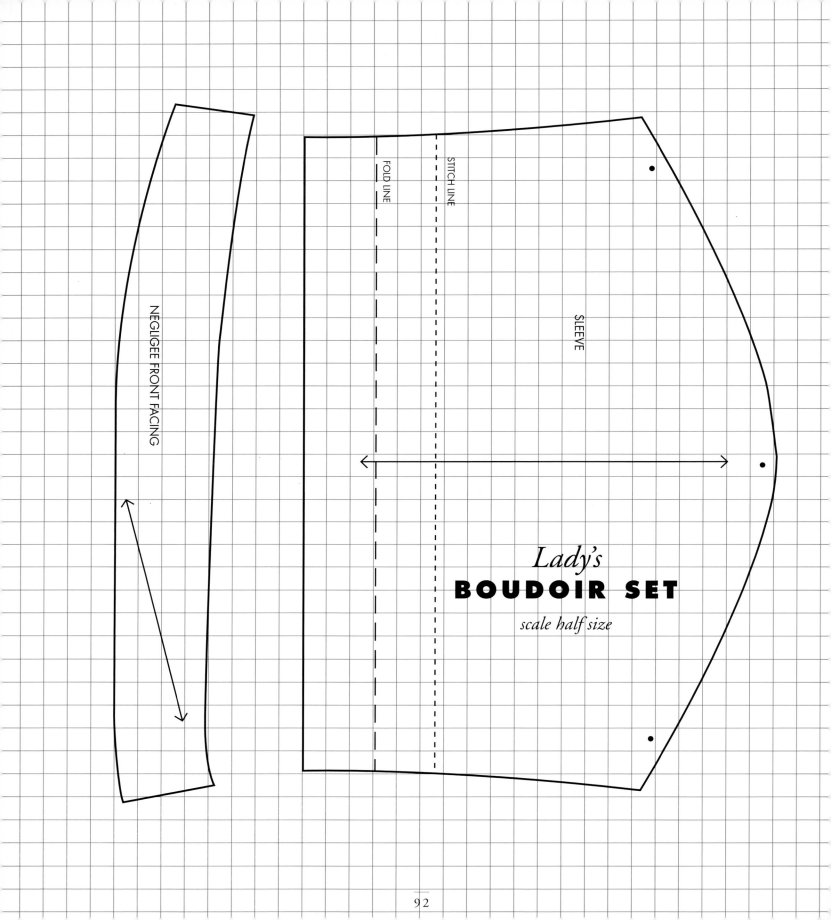

NEGLIGEE FRONT FACING

FOLD LINE

STITCH LINE

SLEEVE

Lady's
BOUDOIR SET

scale half size

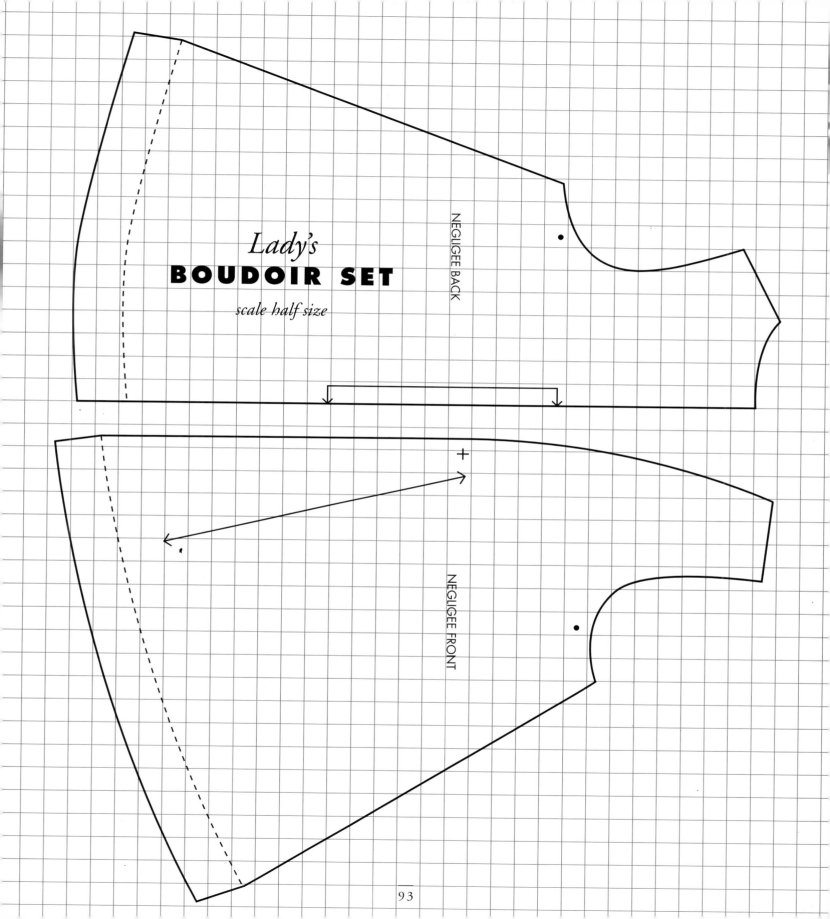

Lady's
BOUDOIR SET
scale half size

NEGLIGEE BACK

NEGLIGEE FRONT

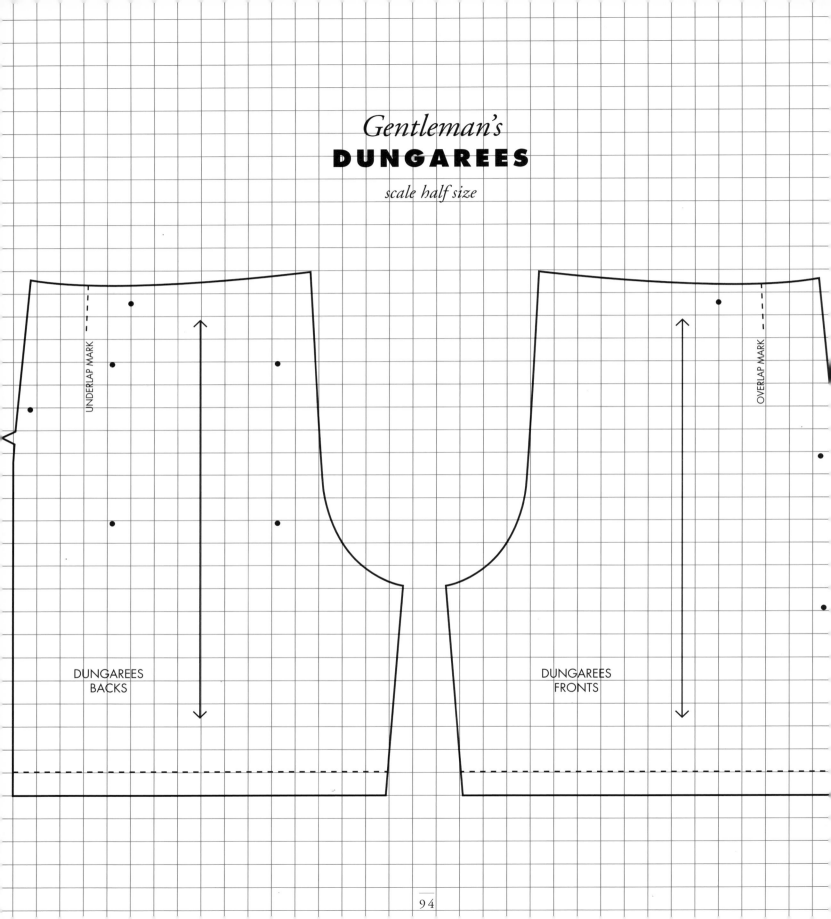

Gentleman's
DUNGAREES
scale half size

UNDERLAP MARK

OVERLAP MARK

DUNGAREES
BACKS

DUNGAREES
FRONTS

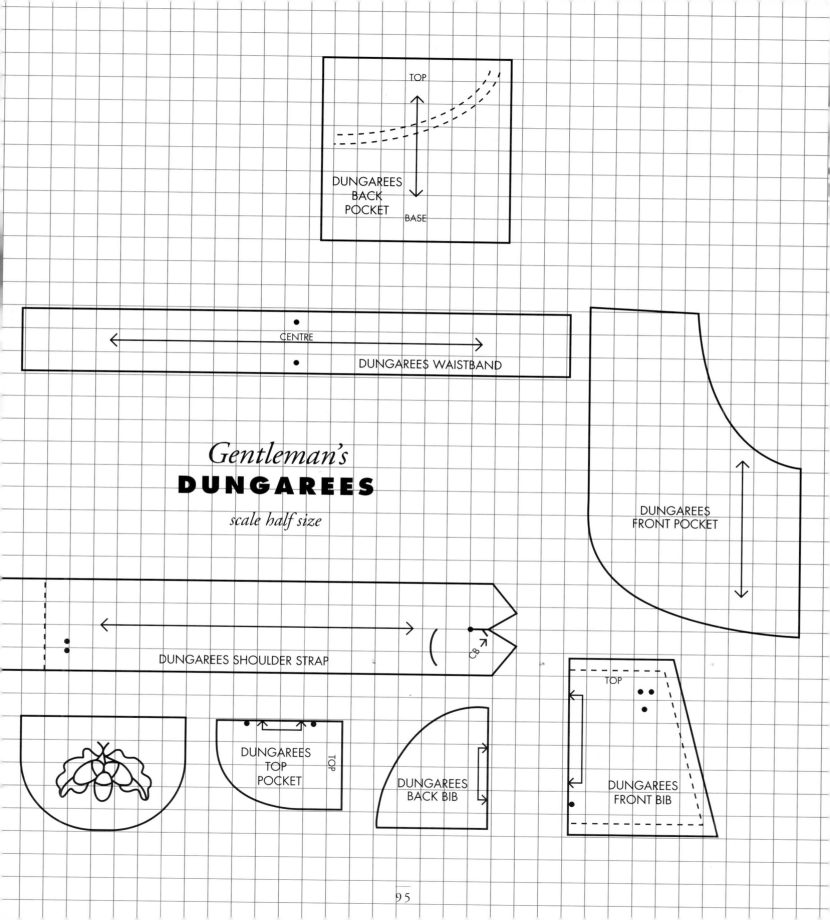

TOP

DUNGAREES
BACK
POCKET

BASE

CENTRE

DUNGAREES WAISTBAND

DUNGAREES
FRONT POCKET

Gentleman's
DUNGAREES

scale half size

DUNGAREES SHOULDER STRAP

CB

DUNGAREES
TOP
POCKET

TOP

DUNGAREES
BACK BIB

TOP

DUNGAREES
FRONT BIB

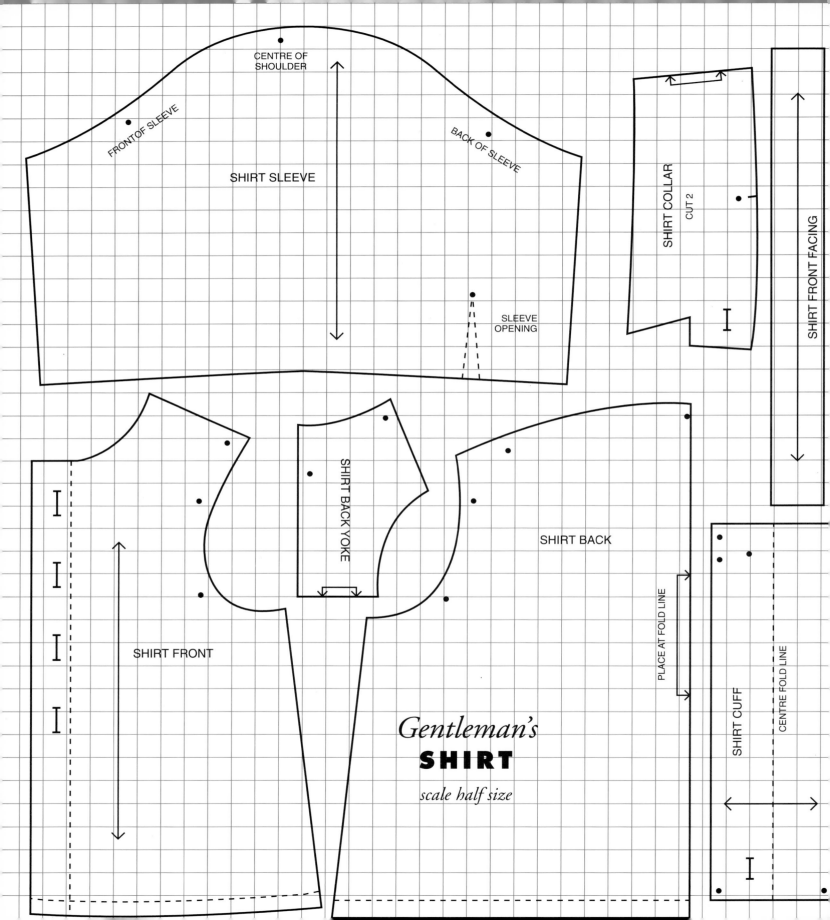

CENTRE OF
SHOULDER

FRONT OF SLEEVE

BACK OF SLEEVE

SHIRT SLEEVE

SLEEVE
OPENING

SHIRT COLLAR

CUT 2

SHIRT FRONT FACING

SHIRT BACK YOKE

SHIRT BACK

SHIRT FRONT

PLACE AT FOLD LINE

SHIRT CUFF

CENTRE FOLD LINE

Gentleman's
SHIRT

scale half size

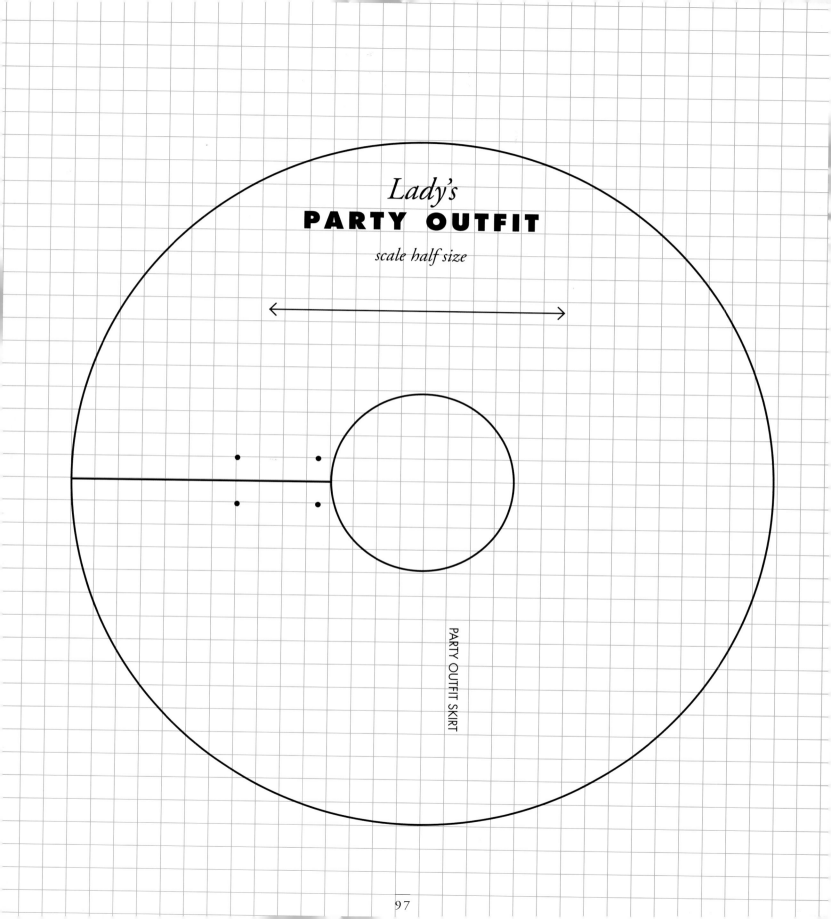

Lady's
PARTY OUTFIT

scale half size

PARTY OUTFIT SKIRT

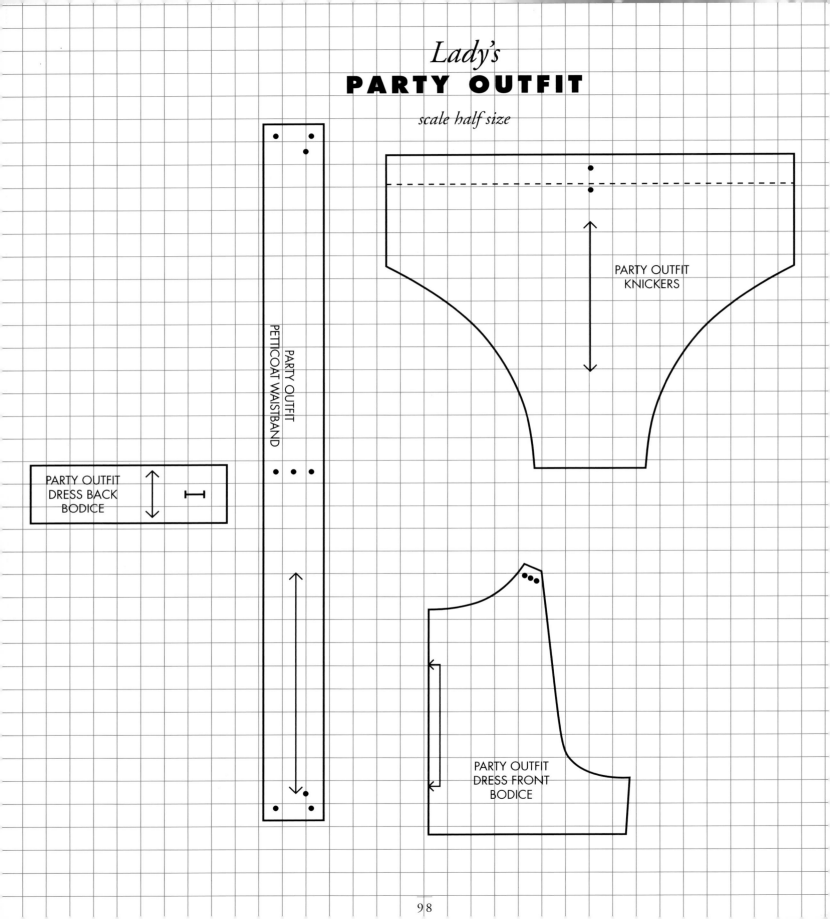

Lady's
PARTY OUTFIT

scale half size

PARTY OUTFIT
KNICKERS

PARTY OUTFIT
PETTICOAT WAISTBAND

PARTY OUTFIT
DRESS BACK
BODICE

PARTY OUTFIT
DRESS FRONT
BODICE

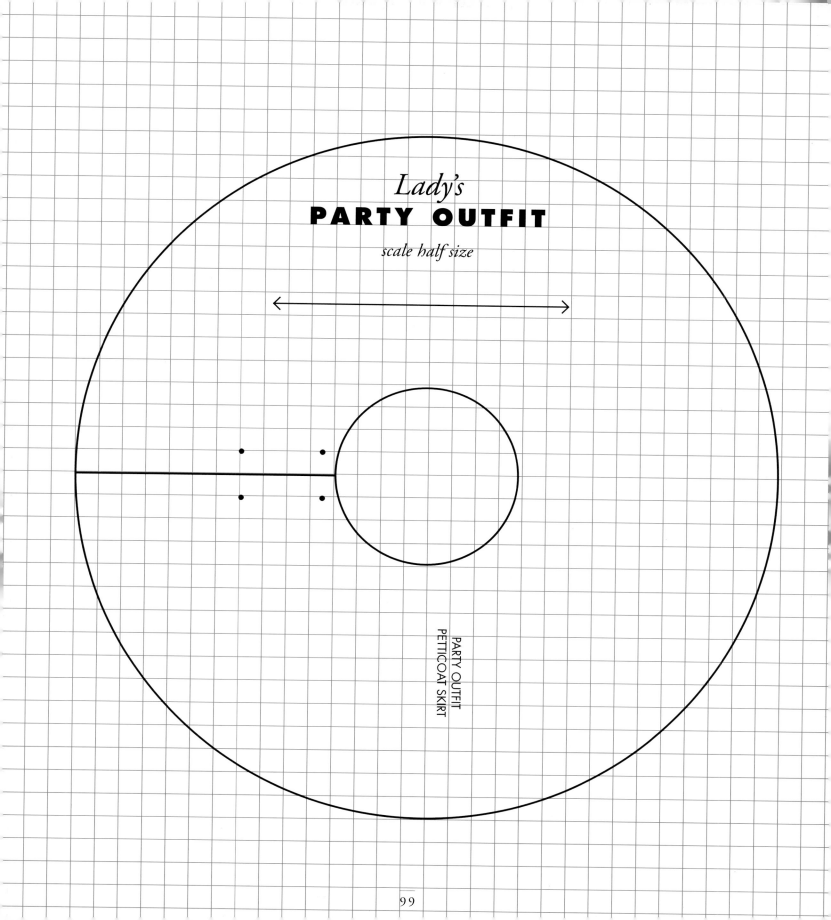

Lady's
PARTY OUTFIT
scale half size

PARTY OUTFIT
PETTICOAT SKIRT

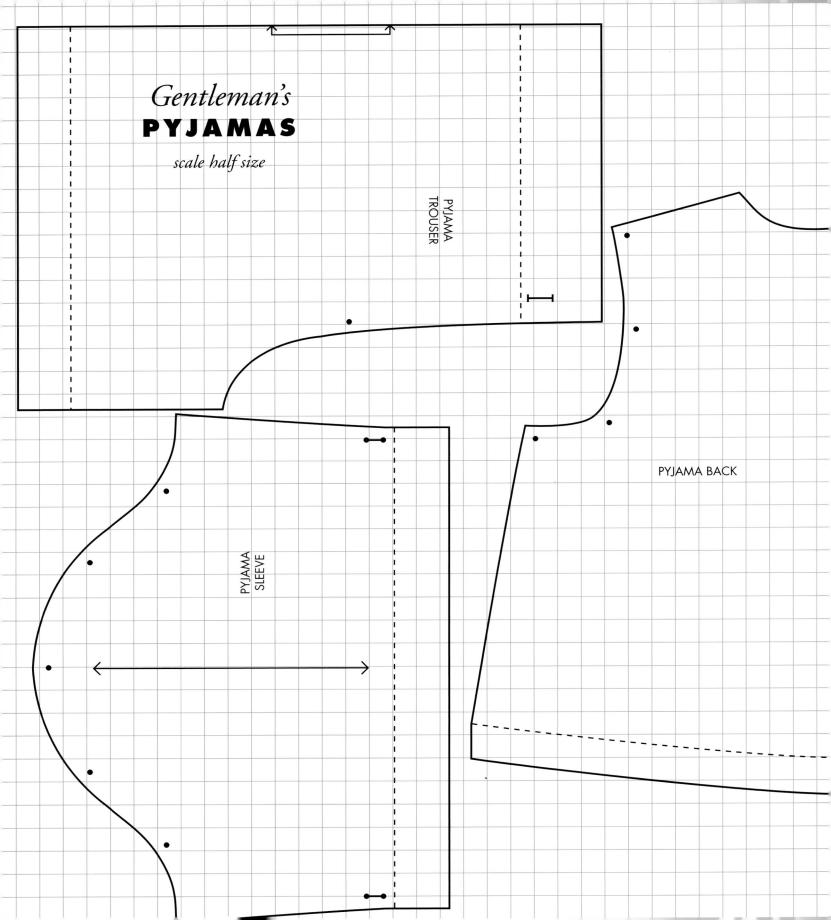

Gentleman's
PYJAMAS

scale half size

PYJAMA
TROUSER

PYJAMA
SLEEVE

PYJAMA BACK

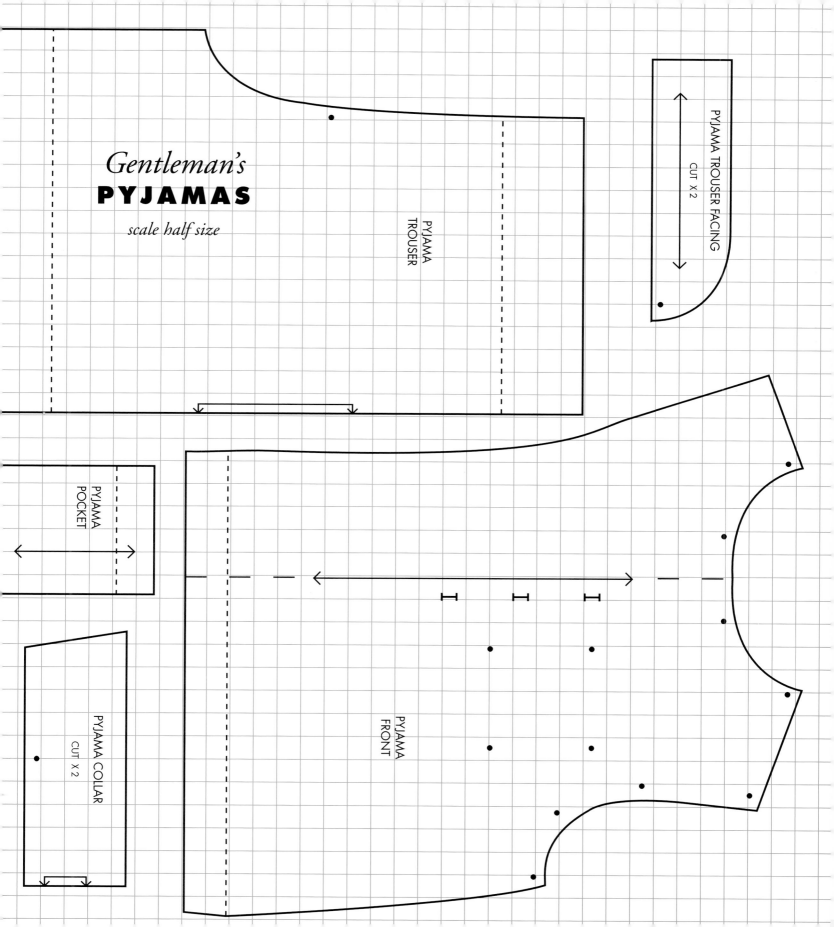

Gentleman's
PYJAMAS

scale half size

PYJAMA TROUSER FACING

CUT x 2

PYJAMA
TROUSER

PYJAMA
POCKET

PYJAMA COLLAR

CUT x 2

PYJAMA
FRONT

FACING

FOLD LINE

COAT
FRONT
BODICE

COAT
BACK NECK
FACING

COAT
BACK BODICE

COAT
BACK BODICE
LINING

Lady's
WINTER COAT
scale half size

COAT
FRONT BODICE
LINING

COAT
SLEEVE
LINING

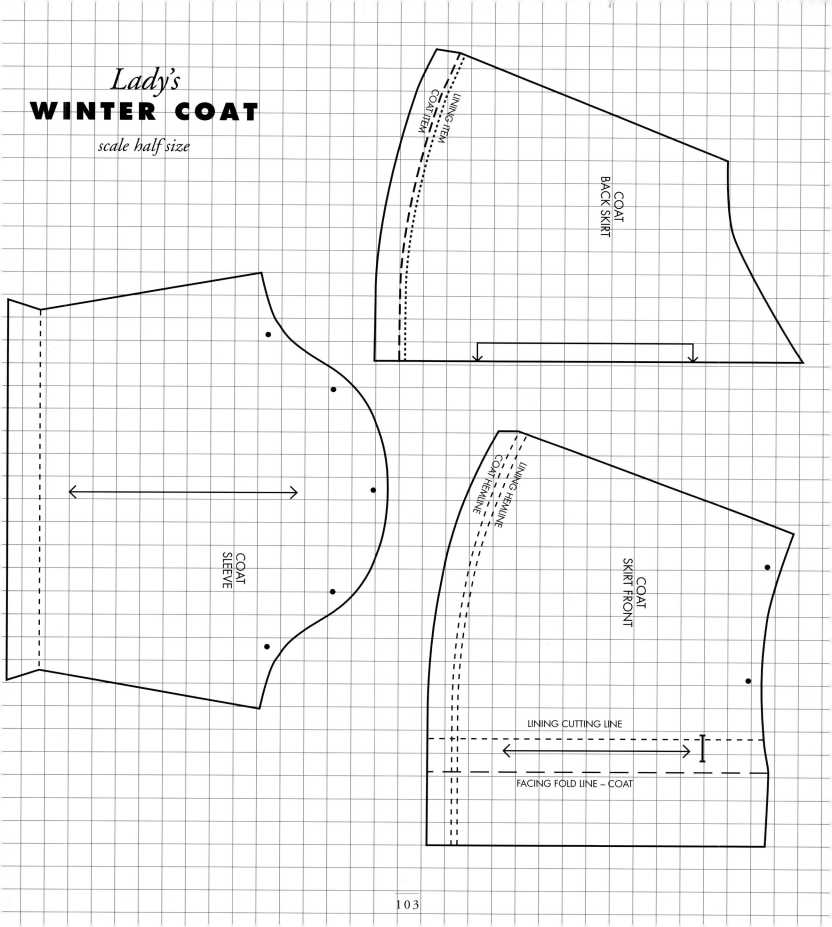

Lady's
WINTER COAT
scale half size

COAT
BACK SKIRT

LINING ITEM
COAT ITEM

COAT
SLEEVE

COAT
SKIRT FRONT

LINING HEMLINE
COAT HEMLINE

LINING CUTTING LINE

FACING FOLD LINE – COAT

103

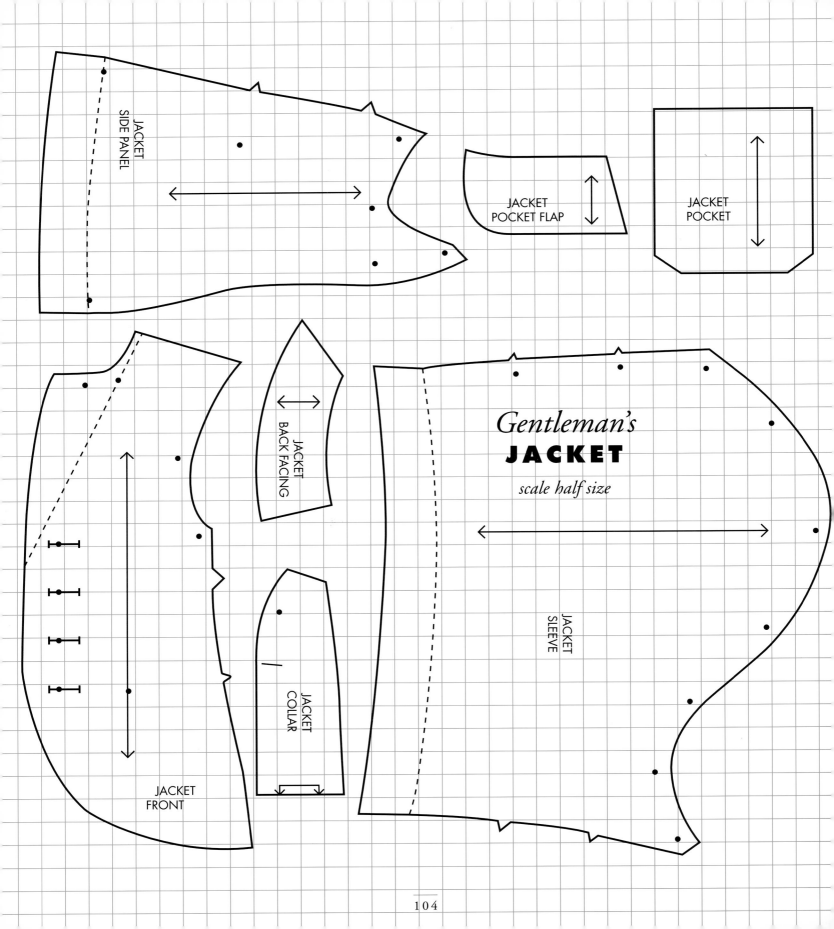

JACKET
SIDE PANEL

JACKET
POCKET FLAP

JACKET
POCKET

JACKET
BACK FACING

Gentleman's
JACKET

scale half size

JACKET
SLEEVE

JACKET
COLLAR

JACKET
FRONT

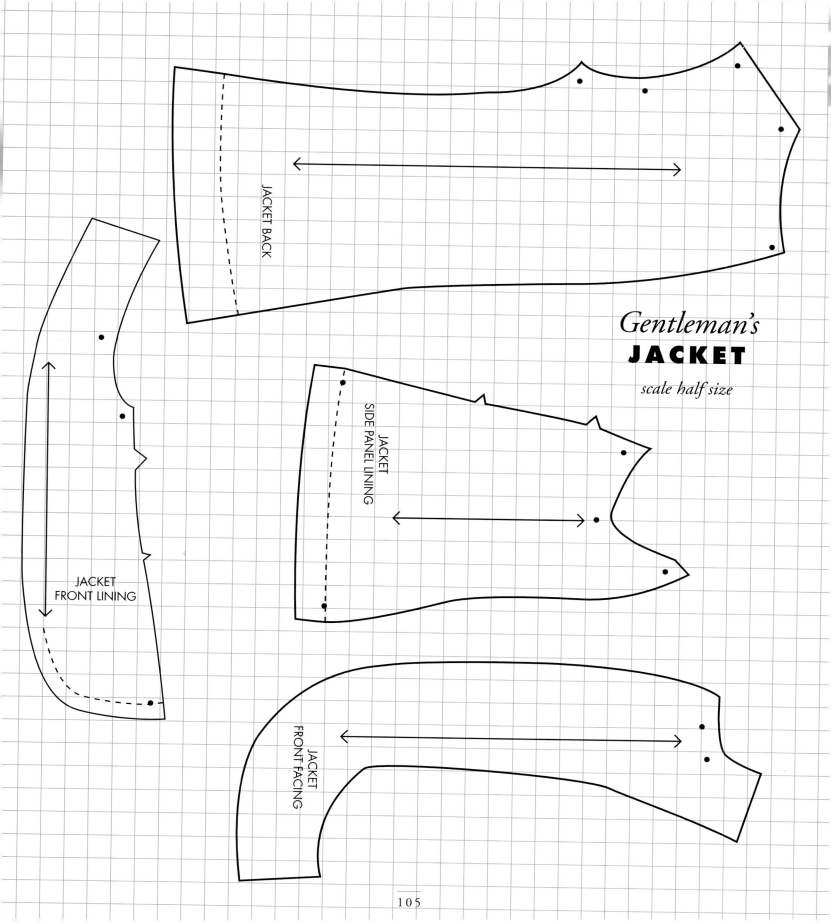

JACKET BACK

Gentleman's
JACKET

scale half size

JACKET
SIDE PANEL LINING

JACKET
FRONT LINING

JACKET
FRONT FACING

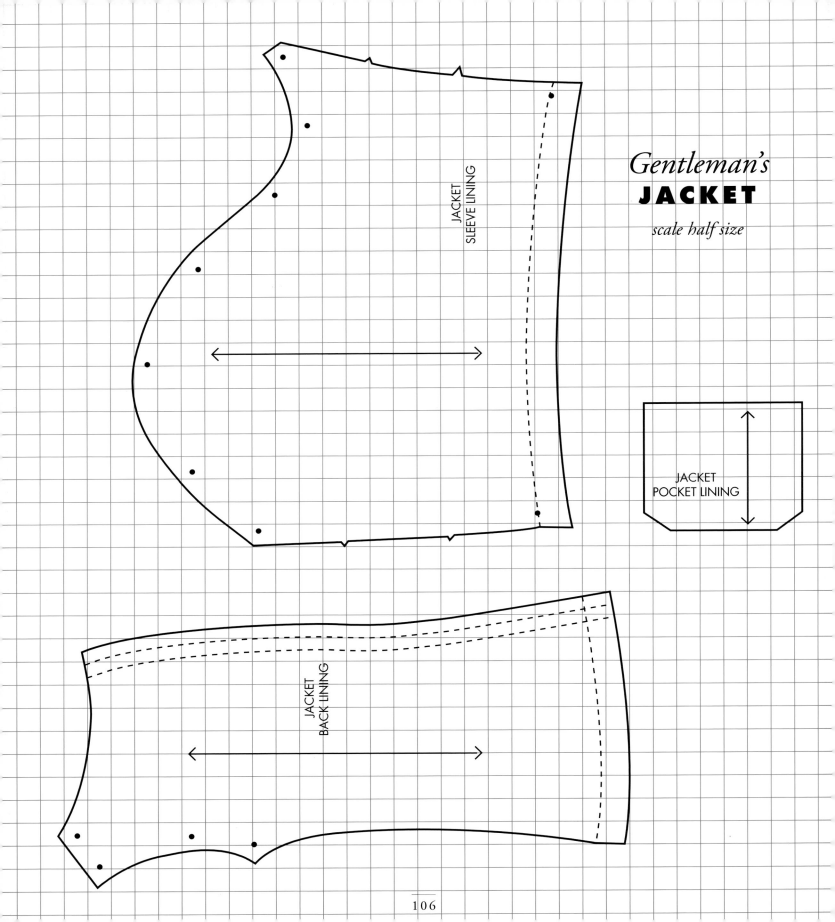

Gentleman's
JACKET

scale half size

JACKET
SLEEVE LINING

JACKET
POCKET LINING

JACKET
BACK LINING

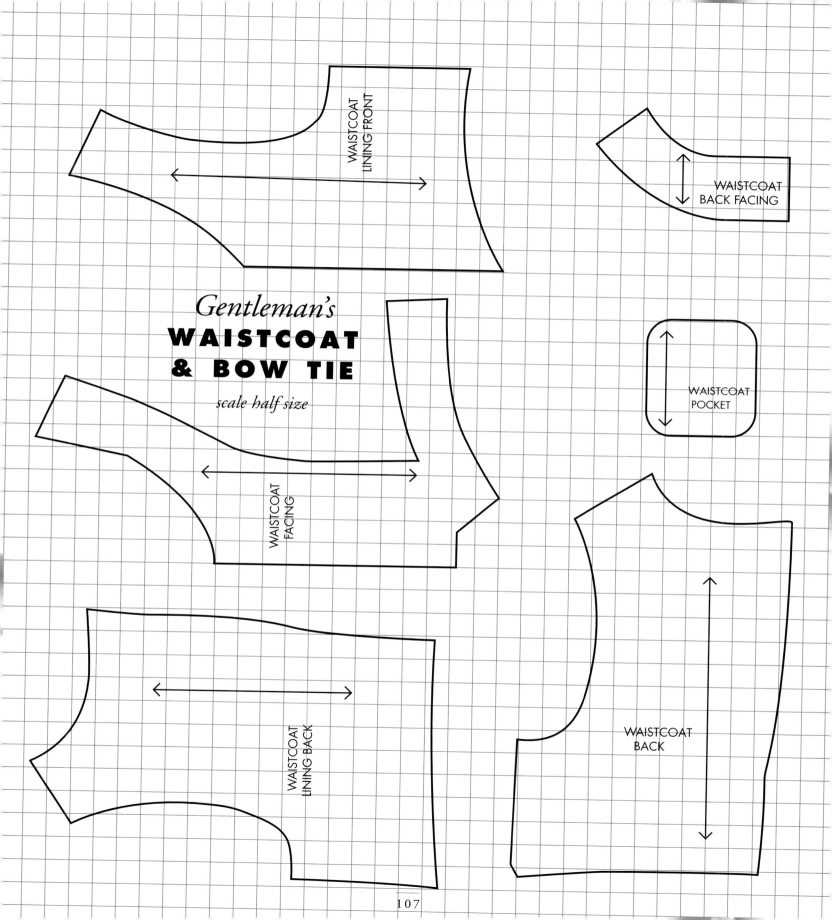

Gentleman's
WAISTCOAT & BOW TIE

scale half size

WAISTCOAT LINING FRONT

WAISTCOAT BACK FACING

WAISTCOAT POCKET

WAISTCOAT FACING

WAISTCOAT LINING BACK

WAISTCOAT BACK

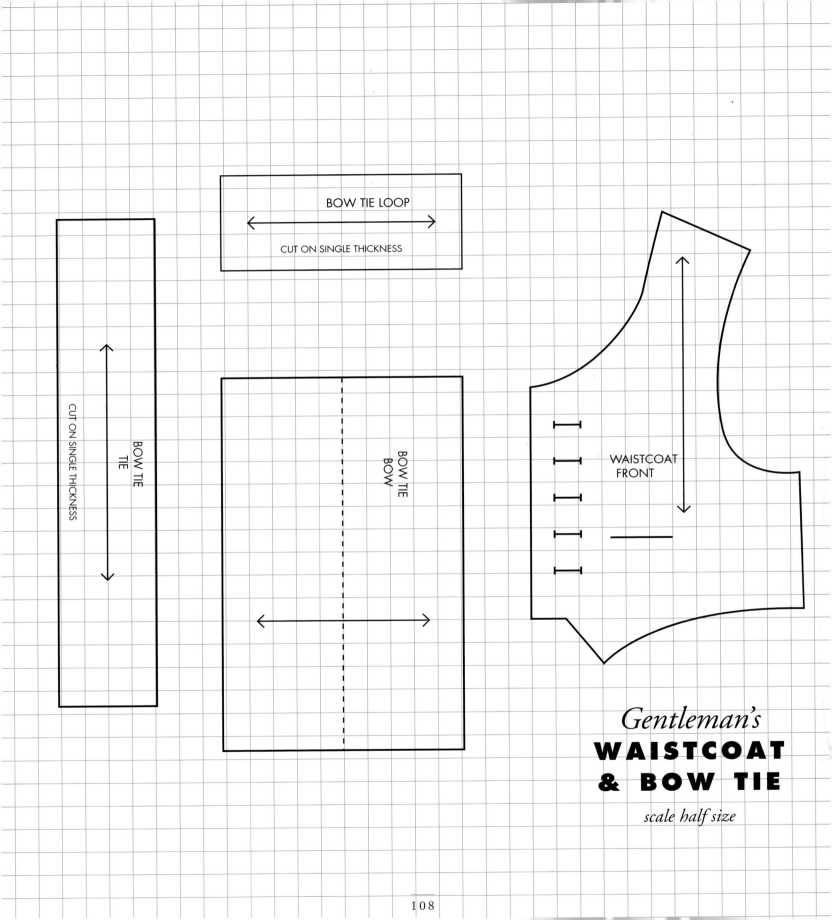

BOW TIE LOOP

CUT ON SINGLE THICKNESS

BOW TIE TIE

CUT ON SINGLE THICKNESS

BOW TIE BOW

WAISTCOAT FRONT

Gentleman's
WAISTCOAT & BOW TIE
scale half size

108

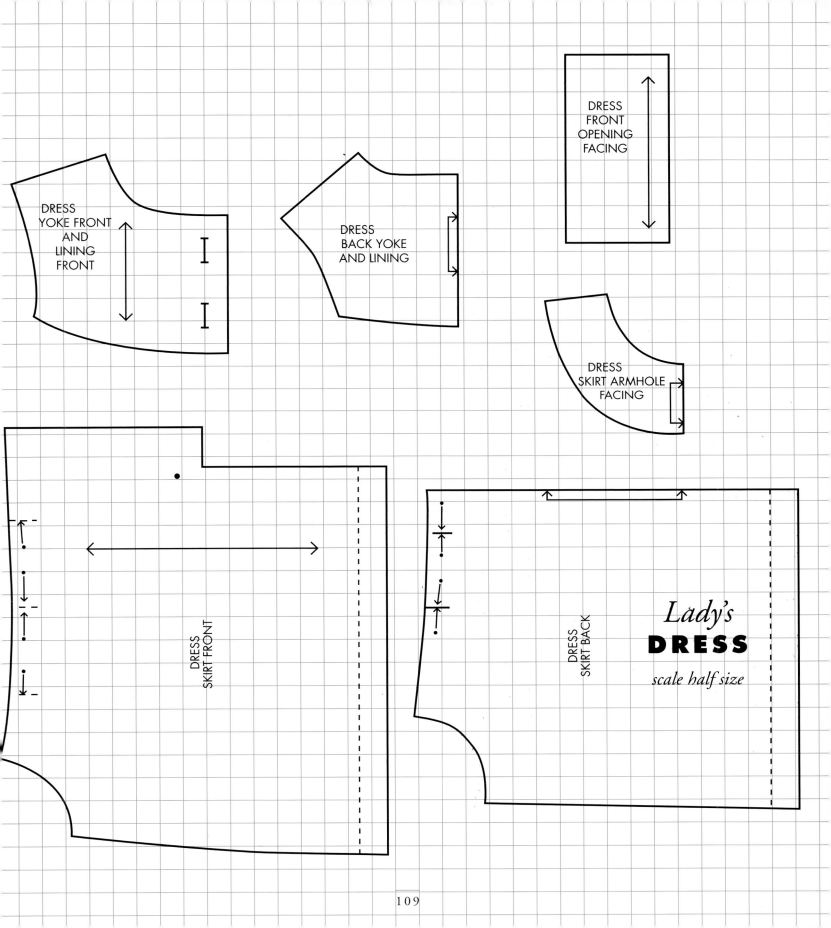

DRESS
YOKE FRONT
AND
LINING
FRONT

DRESS
BACK YOKE
AND LINING

DRESS
FRONT
OPENING
FACING

DRESS
SKIRT ARMHOLE
FACING

DRESS
SKIRT FRONT

DRESS
SKIRT BACK

Lady's
DRESS

scale half size

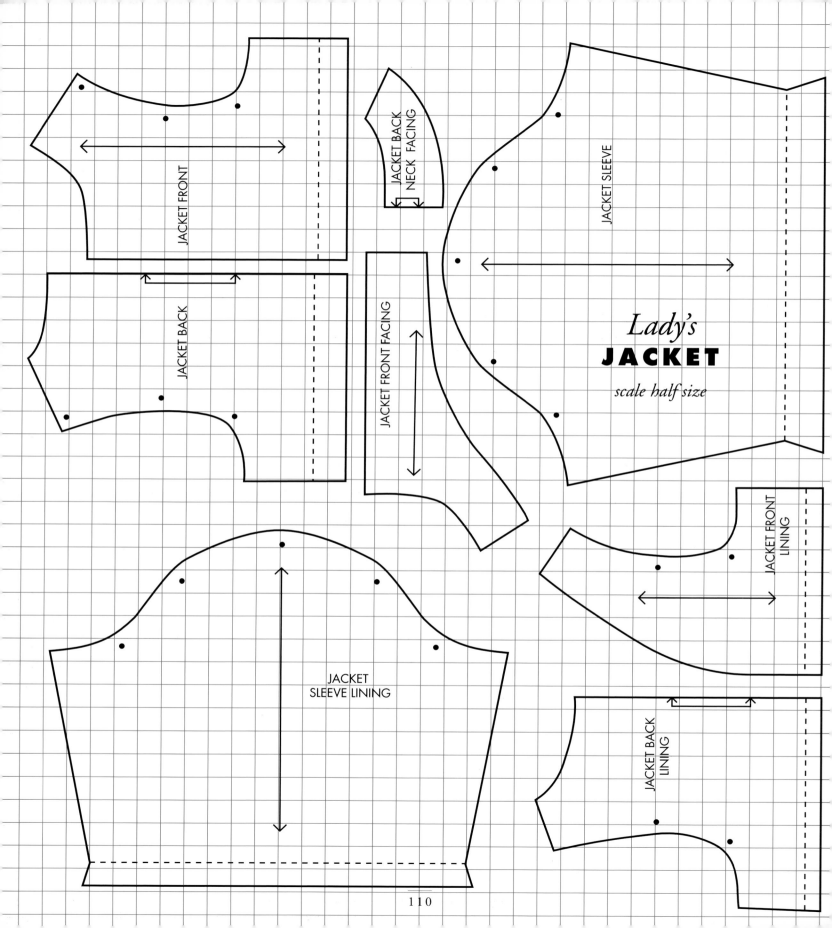

JACKET FRONT

JACKET BACK

JACKET BACK NECK FACING

JACKET FRONT FACING

JACKET SLEEVE

Lady's
JACKET
scale half size

JACKET FRONT LINING

JACKET SLEEVE LINING

JACKET BACK LINING

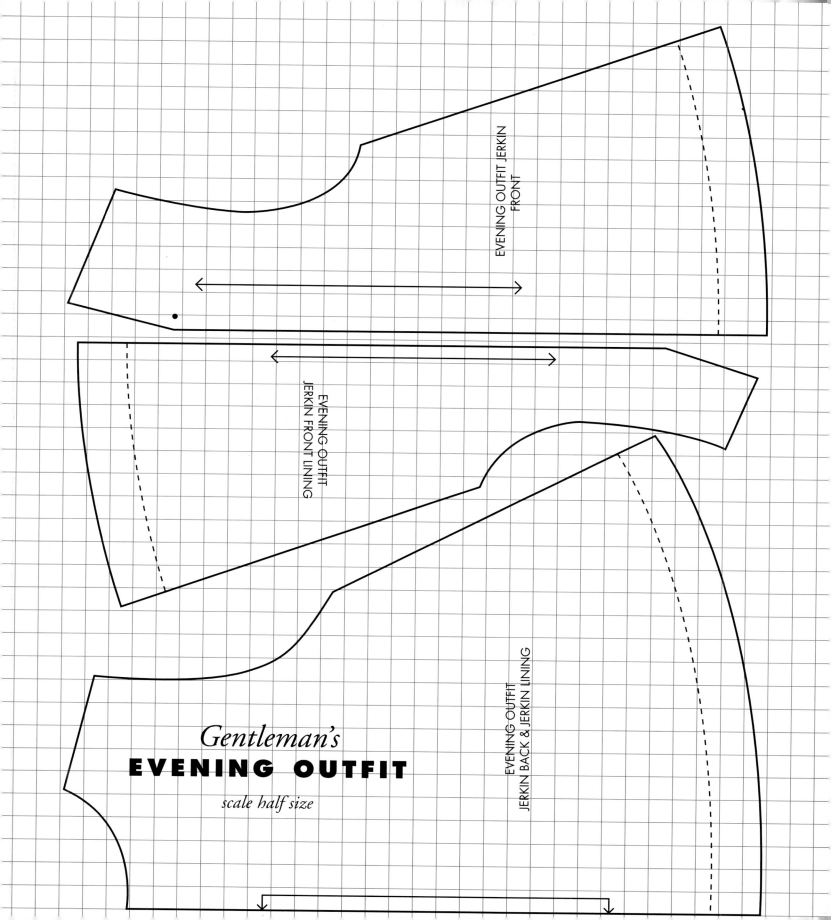

EVENING OUTFIT JERKIN
FRONT

EVENING OUTFIT
JERKIN FRONT LINING

EVENING OUTFIT
JERKIN BACK & JERKIN LINING

Gentleman's
EVENING OUTFIT

scale half size

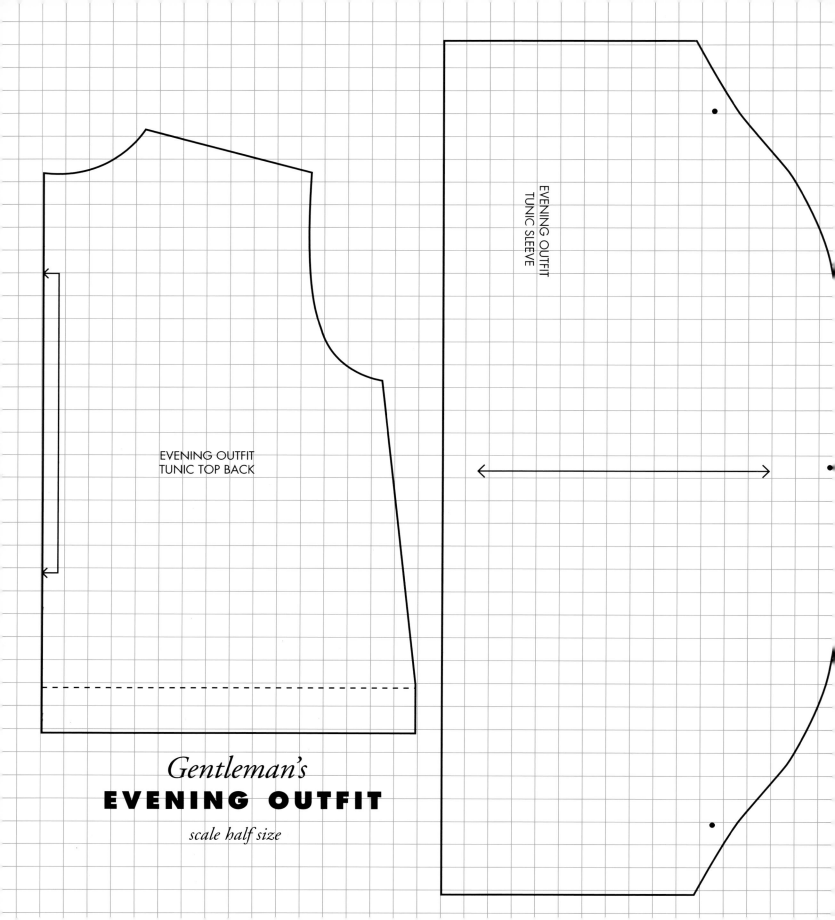

EVENING OUTFIT
TUNIC TOP BACK

EVENING OUTFIT
TUNIC SLEEVE

Gentleman's
EVENING OUTFIT
scale half size

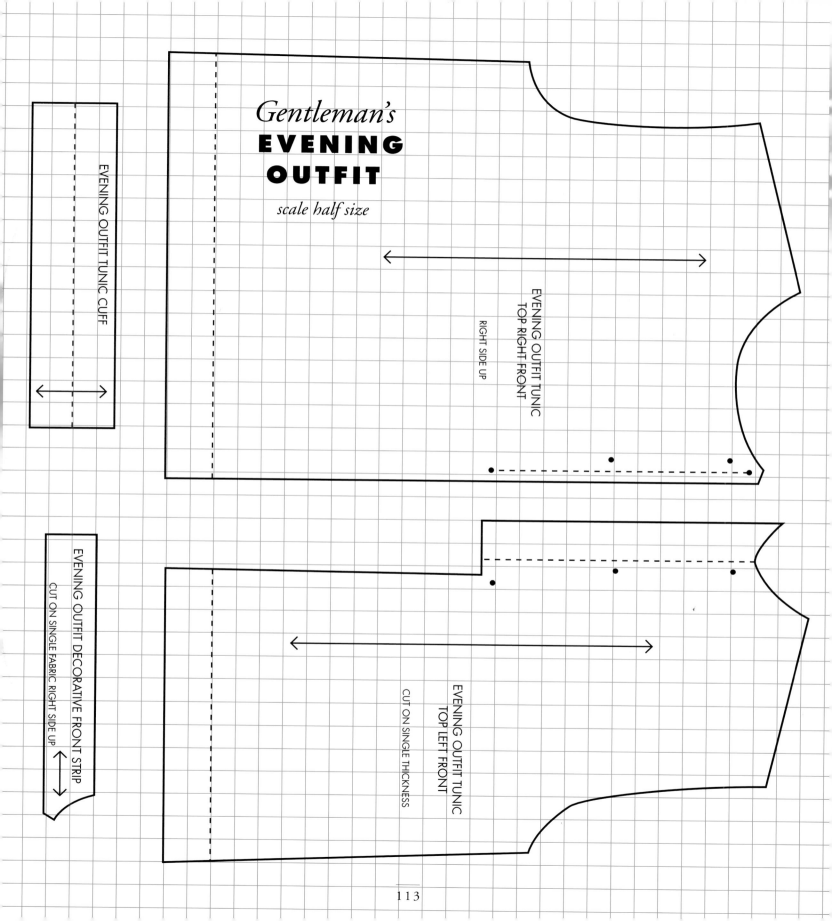

EVENING OUTFIT TUNIC CUFF

Gentleman's
EVENING
OUTFIT
scale half size

EVENING OUTFIT TUNIC
TOP RIGHT FRONT

RIGHT SIDE UP

EVENING OUTFIT DECORATIVE FRONT STRIP

CUT ON SINGLE FABRIC RIGHT SIDE UP

EVENING OUTFIT TUNIC
TOP LEFT FRONT

CUT ON SINGLE THICKNESS

113

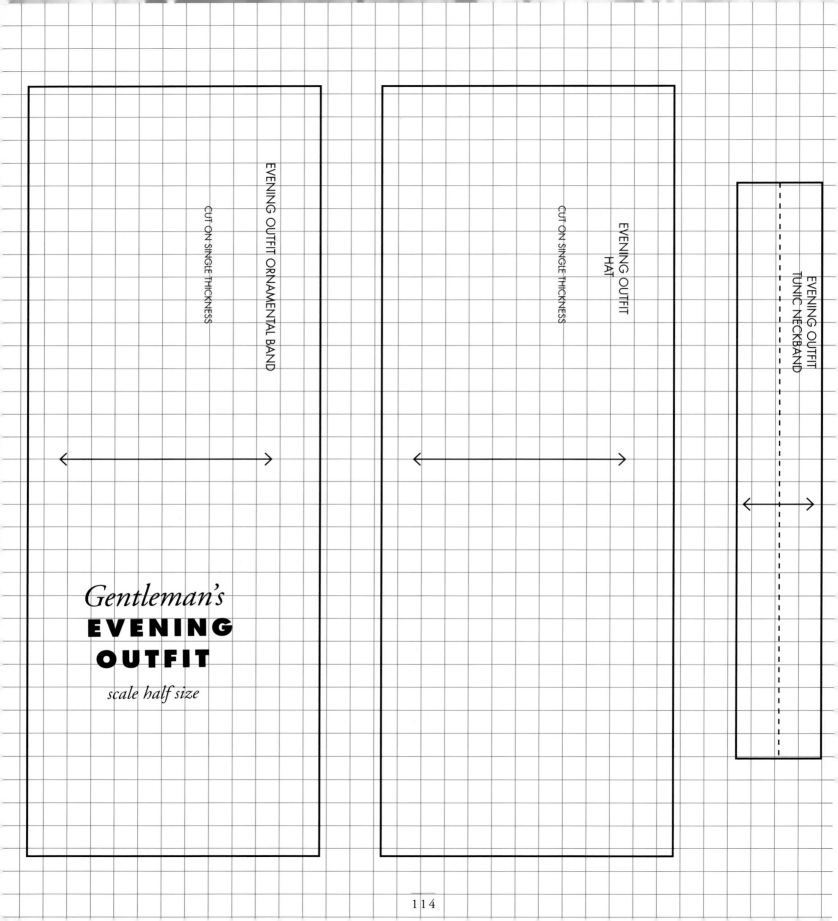

EVENING OUTFIT ORNAMENTAL BAND

CUT ON SINGLE THICKNESS

EVENING OUTFIT
HAT

CUT ON SINGLE THICKNESS

EVENING OUTFIT
TUNIC NECKBAND

Gentleman's
EVENING OUTFIT

scale half size

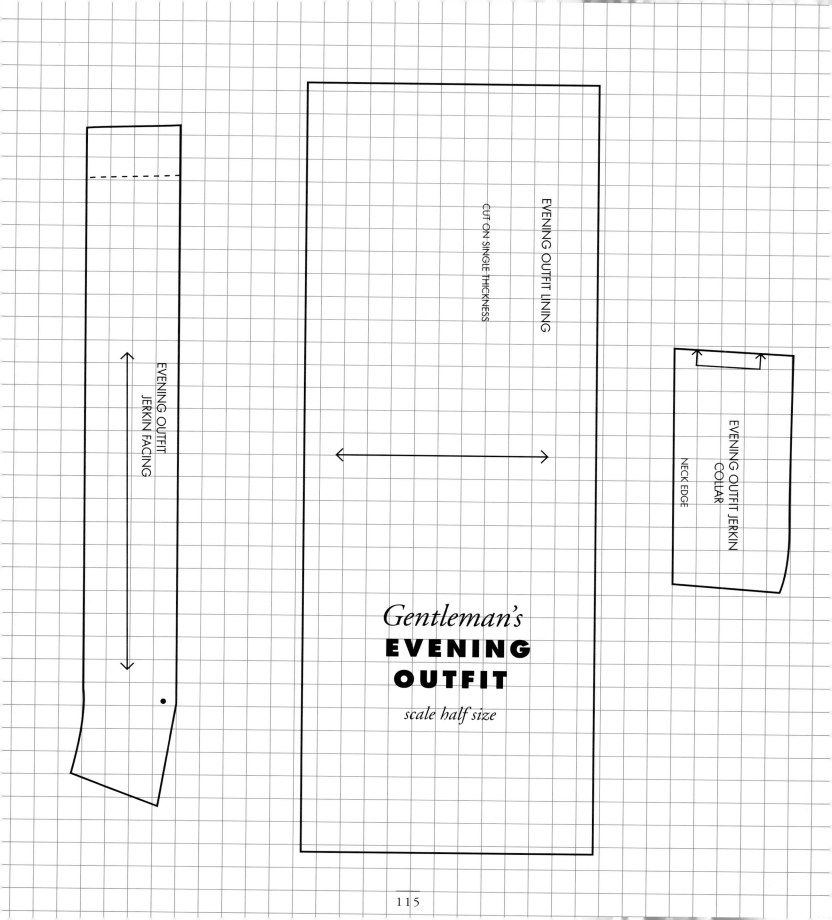

EVENING OUTFIT
JERKIN FACING

CUT ON SINGLE THICKNESS

EVENING OUTFIT LINING

EVENING OUTFIT JERKIN
COLLAR

NECK EDGE

Gentleman's
**EVENING
OUTFIT**

scale half size

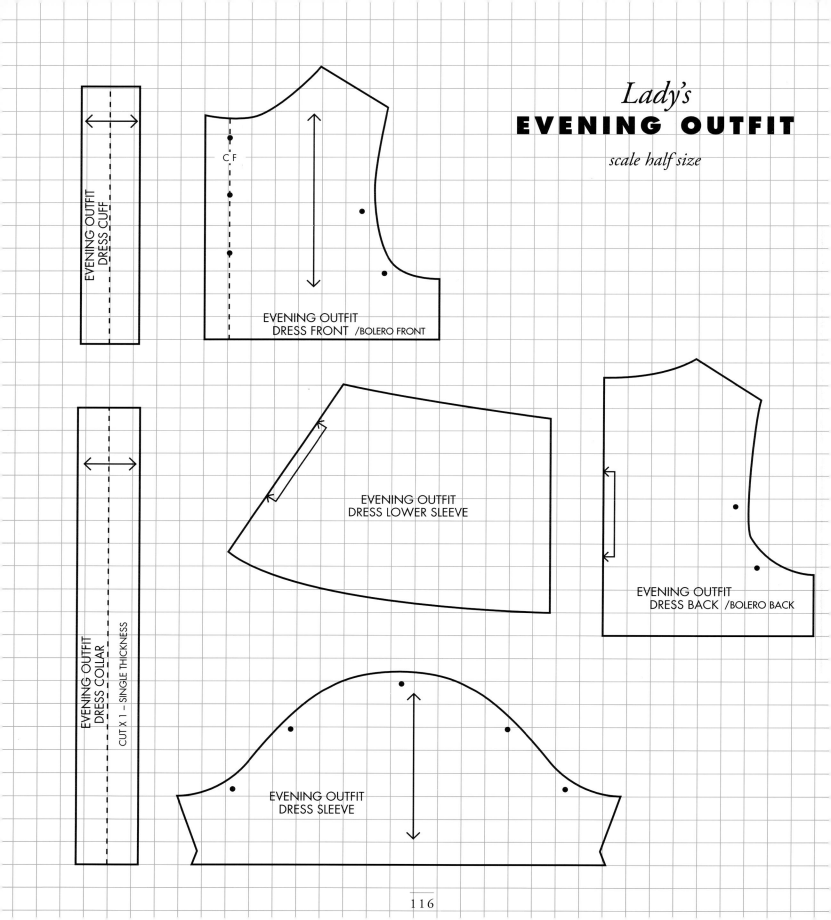

Lady's
EVENING OUTFIT
scale half size

EVENING OUTFIT
DRESS CUFF

C F

EVENING OUTFIT
DRESS FRONT /BOLERO FRONT

EVENING OUTFIT
DRESS COLLAR

CUT X 1 – SINGLE THICKNESS

EVENING OUTFIT
DRESS LOWER SLEEVE

EVENING OUTFIT
DRESS BACK /BOLERO BACK

EVENING OUTFIT
DRESS SLEEVE

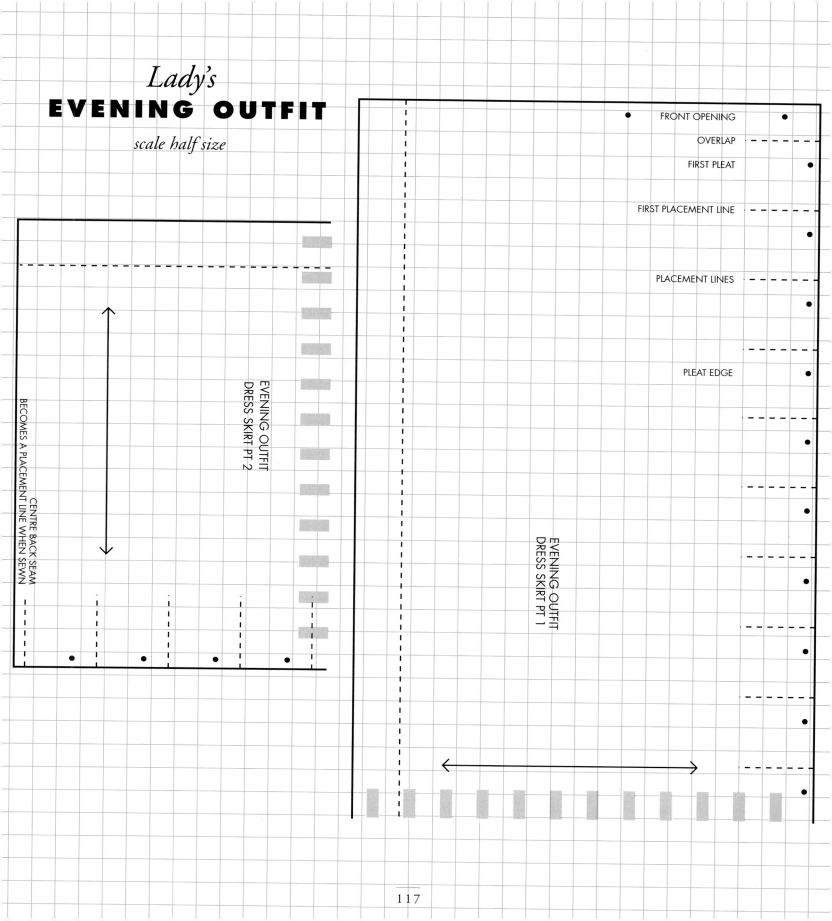

Lady's
EVENING OUTFIT

scale half size

EVENING OUTFIT
DRESS SKIRT PT 2

CENTRE BACK SEAM
BECOMES A PLACEMENT LINE WHEN SEWN

EVENING OUTFIT
DRESS SKIRT PT 1

FRONT OPENING

OVERLAP

FIRST PLEAT

FIRST PLACEMENT LINE

PLACEMENT LINES

PLEAT EDGE

ACKNOWLEDGMENTS

I would like to thank all the staff at Weidenfeld & Nicolson who have worked so generously to produce this book. In particular Beth Vaughan for encouraging me and ensuring everything ran smoothly, including myself. Many thanks go to Alison Wormleighton for her scrupulous copy editing and deciphering of my hand-printed text and to Jenny Hughes for her selfless generosity of time and effort in transforming my diagrams into things of beauty. I would also like to thank Martin Norris who's photographs so enrich the text and for his unfailing professionalism and good humour. I consider myself extremely fortunate to have been able to ask Pam Howells to make the bears featured in this book, and I thank her for providing such splendid models. Also I am especially grateful to Anna and Graham Kinaird for their support and for making all the hangers and clothes stands featured in this book. Finally a thank you to all involved for making it so enjoyable, particularly Tom, Tee-Wi and Pippa for their consistent enthusiasm and to Dorabella herself, without whom this particular book might never have been achieved.

First published in 1997 by

George Weidenfeld & Nicolson

The Orion Publishing Group

Orion House

5 Upper St Martin's Lane

London, WC2H 9EA

British Library Catalogue-in-Publication Data

A catalogue record for this book is available from the British Library

ISBN 0 297 83551 3

Edited by Alison Wormleighton

Illustrated by Jane Hughes

Designed by Paul Cooper

Photography by Martin Norris

Printed and bound in Italy